Safety Monitor

Safety Monitor

How to Protect Your Kids Online

DETECTIVE MIKE SULLIVAN

Naperville, IL Police Department

Bonus Books
Chicago and Los Angeles

06   05   04   03   02   5   4   3   2   1

Library of Congress Control Number: 2002108386

ISBN: 1-56625-1869

Bonus Books
160 East Illinois Street
Chicago, Illinois 60611

Cover design by Mike Stromberg
Cover photo courtesy of Photodisc

Printed in the United States of America

*To Jeanine, Sarah, and Brady, the reasons for this book,
and to Chief David Dial and Sergeant Mark Carlson
who had the vision.*

*Special thanks to David Schippers, Jeff Stern,
Max Lane, and Erin Kahl for without their help
this book would not have been possible.*

Contents

CONTENTS

CONTENTS

PART FOUR **FURTHER RESOURCES**

9   Further Resources   277
     America Online   277
     MSN   282
     Club Tech   285
     Anytime Anywhere Learning Laptop Program   286
     Illinois State Attorney General's Web Site   294
     Other Sites of Interest to Law Enforcement   297

Index   331

Introduction

The world of computing and Internet access is an irreplaceable asset in providing entertainment, education, and access to information. There's simply no better way to find, analyze, and store information, or keep in touch with colleagues, family, and friends.

As with any powerful tool, common sense and safety should be our primary concerns.

We are used to thinking about safety in the physical world. For instance, in the automotive world we lock our cars, license our drivers, monitor their driving records, and prohibit certain activities, such as drug or alcohol usage, before driving.

When it comes to computers and the online experience, the dangers are far less obvious. We feel anonymous, protected, and in control when we are in front of our computers. We feel safe in the homes where we keep our machines.

When we think about computer safety, if we think about it at all, we may consider the long-term effects of the low-level radiation from our glowing computer screens. Or the implications of a slight backache we pick up during long sessions in front of the machine. Or perhaps we worry about viruses and hackers and the damage we can sustain from brilliant manipulators of technology.

The truth is, as a policeman I can tell you that the brilliant manipulators of technology have little interest in wrecking our machines and stealing our data. When I first joined the computer crimes unit I had visions of tracking down these criminals and exposing their nefarious schemes. I thought that most of the cases that would get reported would come from the business sector, as they were the prime targets for hackers and computer thieves. I found out that, for most hackers, cracking into someone's home systems was not very challenging. If hackers went back to the newsgroups, chat rooms, or other forms of computer communication to brag about hacking a home computer, they were scorned and ridiculed by their peers.

For the most part, this was true until the popularity of DSL and cable modems increased. With these news high-speed connections, the hacker is interested in the home machine, but not necessarily for the data in the home computer. He is interested in using the home computer to install his own protection software on the computer to prevent any other hacker from gaining access to your machine.

That's right: they are actually helping you to protect your machine so no one else gains access and makes changes to all the hard work he has done to take over using your machine. He does this so he can use your machine remotely to access the Internet and commit his crimes, without you even knowing he is there. When the violations are tracked, they lead back to your machine.

Until high speed internet access become popular, the average citizen was a small fry in the eyes of the hacker. Our exposure to their viruses, Trojan horses, and data destructiveness turns out to be mostly accidental, simply some additional collateral damage that overspills from the hacker's primary targets. He exploits *holes* (errors in computer codes) to manipulate the computer program to give him important data, or give him access to the entire system. A good site to visit for tips on home security measures and further information on hackers, firewalls, and virus software is *http://www.cert.org/tech_tips/home_networks. html.*

In some cases this is not as difficult as it sounds. One of the more common ways to defeat a system is to use the default passwords that come with it which may not have been changed by the system administrator at the company.

For example, let's say we are operating our own Internet service provider and we are currently up online and growing as we get more and more people to subscribe to our service. However, when the system was set up, the system administrator never changed the default passwords. A hacker comes along and tries one of the default user names and passwords (similar to how you sign on at work or home when you want to access your account).

You put in your user name, or screen name, and then your password. In this example the hacker puts in the user name *anonymous* and then for a password he again uses *anonymous*. The user name and password are the same—it is the default manner for signing onto numerous sites—and the hacker now has access to the system.

Not changing the default passwords is like putting very expensive dead bolt locks on your doors and then leaving the keys hanging in the lock on the outside of the door. After the hacker has entered the system he can check other levels of security and discover if in fact he can make himself the system administrator, in other words the owner of the system. If he can, there is no limit to the destruction he can cause to the system. Or even worse, he can use the system to attack a second system. In this situation the ability to find the hacker becomes infinitely more difficult.

It is the brilliant manipulator that we have the most to worry about. Like the confidence men and grifters of another age, they use deception as their primary weapon.

This type of deception has several names but the most commonly used is *social engineering*. The hacker uses his or her skills of deception to trick the victim into supplying the user names and passwords.

A simple way to do this inside a large corporation is to pose as a member of the information services team for the corporation.

The victim receives a telephone call from the hacker.

HACKER: This is Bill Johnson from IT. How's it going?
VICTIM: (*puzzled*) Fine. You?

HACKER: Great. It sure is busy though. We're updating the system with that new monitoring program.

VICTIM: (*completely confused*) Uh, I don't know if I heard about that.

HACKER: Well you know how the communications work around here.

VICTIM: (*He knows the company could do better.*) You bet. So what's the deal?

HACKER: The system is currently being updated with some new monitoring program to prevent the system from crashing, or preventing you from signing in. Been having trouble signing in lately?

VICTIM: Every time they make me change my password!

HACKER: (*laughs*) Well, this should help. I'm looking at your computer right now and I would like you to sign off and then sign back on. Make sure you save your work in progress before you do this.

VICTIM: (*helpful*) Thanks. Got it.

HACKER: That's odd. I didn't see you come on. Could you please sign off and on one more time?"

VICTIM: (*helpful*) Sure. Okay, how's that?

HACKER: This is very odd indeed, I didn't see you come on. Wait just a second. I want to reset the software here. Okay, would you please be kind enough to do this just one more time, but this time please tell me what you are doing as you are doing it?

VICTIM: (*puzzled, but helpful*) Okay. Now I'm signing off.

HACKER: Great. I can see it this time.

VICTIM: (*trusting*) Okay, I'm signing back in.

HACKER: Oh, shoot. I have two sign-ins. I don't think I loaded the system right. Which ID are you using?

VICTIM: J-S-M-I-T-H.

HACKER: Okay, that's right.

VICTIM: Now should I put in the password?

HACKER: Just a sec. Okay, don't put in your six-digit password 0-0-1-1-0-0. That's the default password. Put in the other one.

VICTIM: (*chuckles*) I didn't know I had two. I use this one. Can you see it?

HACKER: I'm seeing about eight right now. People are coming back from lunch.

VICTIM: S-M-I-T-H-Y.

HACKER: Hmm. Okay, I see it. Great. Hey, I think we're done now. Go ahead and re-sign out and in one last time.

VICTIM: Okay, see it this time?

HACKER: Perfectly. Thanks. I really appreciate your patience and cooperation.

Of course, the hacker has now stolen Jim Smith's user ID and password. The system is now compromised. The hacker will return after normal working hours and use the information he just obtained to victimize the system later. Social engineering is a technique that is not relegated to attacking large systems; it is used to attack individuals also. Using these techniques, the hackers have been able to adopt computer technology to enable them to do more harm over a wider area at a lower cost of time and effort than ever before.

The worst of them target our children.

They use the Internet to create, maintain, and distribute a facade, which, after long practice, they know can confuse and dupe a trusting child. They manipulate, exploit, sexually abuse, photograph, and make trophies of young children.

Naturally, they seek to take every advantage the Internet offers in hiding their true intentions and identities.

For years in our unit, we have been targeting, arresting, and convicting these criminals, and watching them march off to the prison cells they deserve.

But they continue to come out of the woodwork. In fact, the supposed anonymity of the Internet encourages more potential abusers to attack children than ever before. Predators who never in a million years would stalk a child in a public playground, are stalking them in chat rooms behind the protection of a fake screen name, which supplies them with a false sense of security. They feel safe in their perceived anonymity, not realizing just how much information about themselves they are giving away.

Prior to working in computer crimes, I spent time in a narcotics squad working undercover. During that time I found that most people I dealt with never used their real names, very few had telephones, most lived via pagers and public phones, and borrowed or rented vehicles with false identification. It made identifying the predators very difficult.

However, when I moved into computer investigations, one of the very first cases involving a traveler was done via a chat room, private messaging, and e-mail with attachments. The attachments were images, some illegal. The thing that stood out most in my mind at the time was the name of several of the legal images sent. The predator actually sent images of himself attached to the e-mail messages. At the time I thought, "Sweet! This predator is really helping me out by giving me pictures of himself."

Then I was totally blown away when I realized the names of the images attached to the e-mail. The names of the images were actually the first and last names of the predator! At the time I thought, "How hard is this area to work in if the predators are going to give you pictures of themselves, their real names, phone numbers, and home addresses?"

After my time in narcotics I thought I had died and gone to heaven where the predators were going to do a lot of my work for me. I wish it had stayed as easy to identify all predators. In time I would learn that the level of computer expertise of the predator would be directly related to how difficult it would be find and identify him.

This phenomenon created a saying around our unit: "we only catch the stupid ones, the really smart ones we don't even know about yet."

No matter how many criminals we catch, your children, as well as mine, are at risk.

The number of people willing to travel to meet children for sexual encounters, even after all the publicity concerning those that have already been caught, never ceases to amaze me. Our unit and others have received a lot of publicity for the arrests we have made concerning computers, the Internet, and child predators. Yet the predators continue to multiply. And sometimes they astonish you with their swagger and cold confidence.

One Sunday afternoon I signed into a chat room where a rather heated discussion was taking place. Many people in the room were upset that law enforcement, and in particular the Naperville Police Department, was now present in their area (chat rooms and private messaging) and posing as children. They argued that it was wrong for law enforcement to invade their private areas.

The other side of the room was arguing that law enforcement was only interested in anyone who was looking to sexually harm a child. They felt that if you were not trying to have sex with a child you shouldn't have a complaint.

The sides finally agreed that the best thing to do was not talk in a sexual manner or attempt to have sexual relations with any child from Naperville.

This was crime prevention at a level we had never envisioned before. However, it did not stop predators from coming after children and we continued to make arrests. After the arrests, one thing became clear: the predators did not think all the publicity, and the arrests of the other predators, had anything to do with them. They were smarter and had made sure they had covered their tracks. In the end it was their arrogance that lead to their arrests.

No matter how many predators we catch, we want to reach out to you, the parent or educator, and help you understand how to prevent your children from becoming the next victims.

Years of experience have taught me and other members of the law enforcement community not only how to catch these predators, but how families can take common-sense steps to protect themselves against predators.

Using the techniques described in this book, and basic common sense and precautions, there is no reason why you and your family cannot enjoy a safe and rewarding computer and online experience.

Never lose sight of the fact that the predators and their dangers only make up a very small portion of the online experience, in fact a very small part. However the harm they can cause is extremely destructive to their victims and because of that we need to use the tools available to limit, if not completely eliminate, their contact with our children.

So where do we start?

From my experience, I can tell you that many parents need to start by getting to know a little more about their children's computers. Even those of us who have computer experience use our machines in different ways than our kids. For many of us parents, our first significant computer experiences come when we bring home a computer for our kids' education.

I know this was my first experience with a computer. My daughter needed one to keep up in school, and being an earlier model it was quite cantankerous. It liked to crash all the time, take frequent breaks and just stop working for a few minutes, and hide the documents she had created.

I was fortunate that I had my daughter present to help me learn about the computer. At work, our department was modernizing under the direction of a new chief. We would soon all be getting a computer on our desks.

I spent more and more time learning about the computer so I could repair our home computer. At work, I was being sent to schools to learn about the components of a computer, networking, and the Internet. Every day I seem to learn something new and I enjoy the exchange of knowledge with others, either in law enforcement or private industry. I have learned how to take the complexities of computers and make them understandable to the layperson during staff meetings, town hall meetings, public speaking at home owners associations, and teaching at police departments and colleges.

So in this book I have included not just the information on how to protect your children, but how to talk to them about the Internet so they can help protect themselves. Also, there is basic information on computers and the Internet so you can play a full role in supervising your children's online experiences. There is a section on who the predators are and how they can (and do) use the Internet to contact, manipulate, and ultimately exploit your child.

As we begin, remember that every Web site and chat room is like a city park. Most are wonderful places; some are dangerous. You wouldn't send your child to a park without checking it out first. Parental supervision is essential to safe online experiences.

Parental supervision begins with understanding the computer itself, but let me offer first what I call the "Three Nevers of Protecting Children Online."

The Three Nevers

1. **Never forget that information and help is all around you, including law enforcement agencies, schools, and resources like this book.** *There is no such thing as a stupid question when it comes to learning about*

computers, the Internet, and your child's safety. Never be intimidated into not asking a question; not having the information can come back to haunt you.

2. **Never discuss personal subjects with or give out personal information to a stranger online.** *Children understand that Mr. Stranger Danger is the guy in the black overcoat, the one who comes up to them on the playground or in the mall. Unfortunately, this recognition of strangers breaks down on the Internet. In teaching safety classes to children, I have learned that after one or two online chat conversations the stranger is no longer a stranger. The children now refer to the stranger as "my friend online." If you ask them to describe a stranger they will tell you it is someone you have never met, someone who you don't really know who he or she is, and someone with whom you should not talk. Then ask them about their online friend. Have you ever met this person? Do you know what he looks like? Yes, he sent you a picture, but how do you know that is really him in the picture? So if you have never met him and you don't really know what he looks like, even after two or three conversations online, what is he? The resounding yell form forty fourth or fifth graders is "A STRANGER!"*

3. **Never overreact with your children about their online experiences. Your open line of communication with them is more precious than you think.** *Children are very quick to pick up on what will get them in trouble and what won't. They all know that if their par-*

ents find out about certain things they have done they can be in trouble.

Also, they are sharp enough to know that some things are better heard from them rather than from strangers. They will be in less trouble if they tell their parents instead of letting the word of what they did get to Mom and Dad from a neighbor or the clerk at the store.

But they are equally as quick to realize that if they tell Mom and Dad, they might be punished severely. Avoid this if you can. Make sure your children know that if there is a mistake they can tell you about it without it being an international disaster.

They need to know they can come to you when they have a problem and you will help them and not just punish them. This open communication will pay off dividends all through your life.

Throughout this book you will also find Detective Mike's Laws. These are straightforward rules of the road that I have found true and valuable to remember. You will find them at the beginning of every chapter, but here they are collected in one place.

1. *Never talk to strangers, particularly online. Files and programs are strangers, too.*
2. *Nothing is more important in protecting your children than helping your children to protect themselves.*
3. *If you want to play major-league ball, you need a major-league mitt. Use strong protection at all times.*

4. *One determined parent is more than a match for the individual predator.*
5. *Everything that is digital can be manipulated and everything on a computer is digital.*
6. *The increase in danger is proportional to the number of devices you have, divided by the time you spend educating your children about them.*
7. *What matters is not how you control your online experience, but who. Namely, you.*
8. *Treat your connection to the Internet like the door to your child's bedroom, and watch the traffic accordingly*

At the end of the book, you will find a list of groups you can contact or join, Web sites you can visit, and software you may wish to look into.

This is absolutely everything I can think of that you will need to learn about the computer basics, learn about predators, learn about protecting your children, and learn about places you can go for more help.

The rest is up to you. It starts with a little bit of learning, common sense, and then a great deal of open communication. Sit with your children, surf with them, and enjoy the time with them, for all too soon they will be the ones worrying about their children. There's nothing better than really talking with our children.

DETECTIVE MICHAEL SULLIVAN

How to Use this Book

This book was prepared not only for the experienced online parent, but for the novice. Too many times I have met parents who have the sincere desire to protect their children from online predators, but lack basic familiarity with computers and the Internet.

Part Three, "Understanding the Computer and the Internet," was developed for these parents and educators. While not a substitute for computer and software manuals, it is designed as a primer for basic understanding of the tools and terms used in the online environment. By reading this section, or its individual chapters on online software, peripheral devices from printers to modems, or the basic operating system, you'll get the knowledge you need to supervise your child.

I have kept the use of technical jargon to a minimum,

but if at any time you begin to feel uncomfortable with the terms and concepts, please review Part Three!

Note on Opinions and Recommended Products

The opinions in this book are mine and are not meant to be expressed as those of the City of Naperville or the City of Naperville Police Department. They are based on my experience working in computer crimes and seeing what the predators do to our children. They are also based upon my experience with the software I have recommended because I use the software and feel a sense of security for my children in using it.

I have not received any payment by the companies to use their products or recommend them in this book. They are products I was using long before I ever had an idea to write this book, and the only compensation for those products were versions of the product for use and evaluation.

One other product that was instrumental in the creation of this book was Paint Shop Pro by Jasc Software of Eden Prairie, Minnesota. Their software made all the images you see in the book and all the slides in the Safekids PowerPoint presentation possible.

PART ONE

The Online Predator ▶

Understanding the Online Predator

OVERVIEW

What You'll Learn

- How harassment and abuse is directed at your family via the Internet.
- How the predator plans, thinks, works. What his weaknesses and fears are, and how to use his own weaknesses against him to protect your child.

How You'll Feel

- Horrified at some of the examples of predator abuse, but confident that active parenting can protect your child. (And make no mistake: active parenting is required!)

What Is Covered

- E-mail harassment
- Spam from online pornographers
- Death threats
- Harassment via postings with newsgroups and bulletin boards
  —How to check if offensive misinformation is published on the Internet about yourself or your child
- Graphic child pornography via e-mail
- Contact from online predators
  —Protecting our families: first steps
- The traditional predator
- The online predator
- Online predators and chat rooms
- How the online predator makes his first approach
- How a predator lures your children
- How a predator uses addresses, names, and hobbies
- How online predators use videoconferencing
- The key questions predators ask of your children
- Why there are so many predators out there
- "The Three Nevers of Online Child Protection"
- When and how you should notify authorities about a possible predator
- Free speech rights and limits of police protection

> ## Detective Mike's First Law
>
> *Never talk to strangers, particularly online.*
> *Files and programs are strangers, too.*

1 Types of Online Abuse of Children (And Adults)

Abuse and threats to our children take many forms, and all of them are important to know about and protect ourselves against. Threats to safety on the Internet can include:

▶ 1.1 E-mail harassment

It is very common today that children receive e-mail of a harassing nature. Most of the e-mail is junk mail or can be attributed to friends or classmates. The most common type of e-mail is the one threatening to kick your child's butt if he or she does not stay away from this boy or this girl in school.

Unfortunately, one popular television show contains scenes in which one character goes out to a Web site each day and updates the "School News." In a television show where there are no real victims this may seem like a "cute" thing to do. However, in the real world it is not cute to post all the names of the gay students, for example, to a Web site. School systems across the country are dealing with this type of situation. If the child does not post the information to the Web site using school equipment can they still be disciplined by the school?

In most towns and cities, the schools have the authority to suspend. Additionally, depending on the jurisdiction, the report of such action from the school to law enforcement can be viewed as a criminal matter. Such actions may fall within the disorderly conduct statutes or under laws against ethnic intimidation. The latter is a felony in some states.

Most of the cases of this sort that I have been involved in turn out to be jealous students and they are fairly easy to identify. However, when it happens to your child, you want to be able to make sure it is something as innocent as a jealous student and that it will not lead to anything further. In most cases, the identification of the offender and an interview of the offender and the parents puts the matter to rest. Later in this book you will learn of some software that will help you prevent your child from ever seeing this type of mail.

▶ 1.2 Spam from pornographic Web sites

Extremely common and annoying. This is probably the bulk of the complaints received by most police departments. The advertisement suggests that they have nude pictures of the youngest teens, or even younger children. The advertisement makes it seem that the site is actually engaging in child pornography. However, the images are of adults posing as children. It is an advertising scheme designed to lure people to the site with the youngest, barely legal images.

In the near future, this type of spamming will probably

include the terms "digital" or "simulated" in an effort to conform with the recent rulings of the United States Supreme Court. The fact is that a very low percentage of these sites are dealing with illegal images. Once those illegal sites are identified, they are quickly sent to the U.S. Postal Inspectors, U.S. Customs or the Federal Bureau of Investigation's Operation Innocent Images. Some of these agencies have been dealing with this problem for decades and have procedures in place to route the complaints to the proper agencies in the proper country.

If you are highly concerned, look to your Internet service provider (ISP) first. Do they have spamming controls available for use? Report the abuse to your service provider and maybe they can block the origination point of the spam.

Most ISPs do not allow spamming on their systems and will be more than willing to help you confront the problem. ISPs such as America Online have several different ways of helping you combat spam and their help online is only too willing to walk you through the controls available.

Also, you can use products like Spam Killer, a program designed to help your computer eliminate spam, offered by McAfee.com. This program bounces back spam in a way that suggests your e-mail address is incorrect and your e-mail address is removed from the list.

▶ 1.3 Death threats e-mailed to a teacher or student

Death threats should be taken very seriously in the wake of the tragedy in Colorado. Parents are wary of any type of threat directed towards their child. Most of the threats can be categorized as the type of material we discussed in harassing e-mail. However, there are e-mail threats that must be taken seriously.

In one case, several students in England were planning to kill several of their fellow students and some of the teachers. The plans were discussed over the Internet and one of the students made the mistake of using the school system to send e-mail containing details of the plans. The school system was running software called Policy Central which monitors the school system for key words or phases. The software alerted authorities to the plan and it was stopped immediately. This type of software is available to the police and in Section Two, "Protecting Your Child," we will discuss these products in greater detail.

For now, just keep in mind that when you receive such a threat, print the threat out so you can give the authorities a copy of the full message. This means not only the body of the message, but also who sent the message and the date and time it was sent. The most important information will be found in the header section of the e-mail.

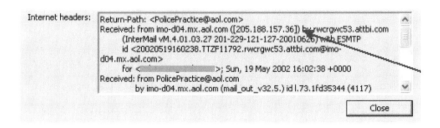

Give this information to the authorities and they can go about identifying who actually sent the message.

▶ 1.4 Harassment via newsgroups and bulletin boards

Most of us are familiar with the Internet and the World Wide Web. We are used to the areas we can surf to and ask questions and get immediate response to our inquiries. However, most have not surfed out to the Newsgroups and seen what exists there.

The Usenet is an older version of exchanging information and is not a real time exchange format. The Usenet is more like the large bulletin boards at your local grocery store. Depending on how you allow your newsreader to view the newsgroups, there can be anywhere from twenty thousand to one hundred thousand newsgroups listed. After I send my post I wait to see who replies to the message. In some cases your newsreader may be your browser such as Netscape, the built in reader for America Online, or an e-mail program like Outlook, or a third party newsreader like Free Agent.

Depending on the program you use, and the protocols used by your ISP, you will be able to access a certain number of these newsgroups. Your ISP may have reservations about some of the newsgroups and therefore will not allow them to be viewed using their software.

The problem that ISPs are dealing with is that newsgroups, like the Internet, are international in scope. There are countries that do not have laws against child pornography and will allow groups such as "Pedophilia—boys" or "Pedophilia—children" to exist. Now, just discussions of the topic may be protected, but images of children, infants to preteen, engaging in sexual content may also accompany the discussion. Again, this content maybe illegal in your country, but as long as the content stays on the machine in the foreign country without laws against this type of material, there are no laws being broken.

However, when someone surfs out to these groups, finds the images, and brings them back to his own machine (downloads them), then in most states he has committed a felony. In most states, child pornography is considered contraband. That means it is illegal to possess child pornography for any reason, unless you are a law enforcement officer or court officer performing your duties. This is similar to the possession of heroin. There is no acceptable use of the drug and it is considered contraband. The mere possession of it is a felony.

In one case that I worked on, the family found that several posts to various newsgroups had been posted to the Usenet. Upon investigation, we discovered thirty-eight postings regarding the father and his daughter.

The first few posts related that the father of the family was rather well endowed, was gay or at least bi-sexual, and was looking for male partners.

Later, postings related that Jennifer (not her real name) was available for sex acts and photographs. Real telephone numbers were included. The family began getting calls at all hours of the day and night from middle-aged sounding men asking for Jennifer. The parents were alarmed, because Jennifer was their nine-year-old daughter. They contacted their local police. The bad guy turned out to be a next-door neighbor who was mad at the family and decided this was how he was going to get back at them. In this situation, the family had done nothing online to warrant the harassment, yet they were victims nonetheless.

1.4.1 How to check if offensive misinformation is published on the Internet about you or your child

How often have you thought to go out and look at what is published about yourself on the Internet? It is easy to do and can reveal interesting results.

First, select a search engine that will make the job most effective. For this purpose we are going to use Google. Type in the Web site *www.google.com* and when it loads, notice just above the search box are the tabs: *Web*, *Images*, *Groups*, and *Directory*.

For this demonstration we will only deal with the first three tabs. If I were to type in the search box the name

Michael Sullivan

I would receive 812,000 hits.

That's way too many to start searching through. I want to find a way to make the search more efficient. By understanding a few simple search parameters I can narrow down the results quickly to find what I am looking for.

In this search, I have asked the search engine to find all pages with either Michael or Sullivan on the page. That's not a very effective way to search. By adding the "+" sign in front and more data

(e.g. **+Michael+Sullivan+Naperville+Police**)

the search engine is told to find pages that have all those words on the page.

Now we have come down to 694 hits, a much more manageable search return. By putting in

"Michael Sullivan"+Naperville+Police"

I get twenty-seven hits, a far cry from 812,000 hits.

The use of quotation marks tells the search engine that these words must be right next to each other on the Web page, thus cutting the search down even further.

I can then review the sites by clicking on each one and reading it.

Finally, let's move over to the groups and search the newsgroups. Searching for

Michael Sullivan

I get back 73,700 hits.

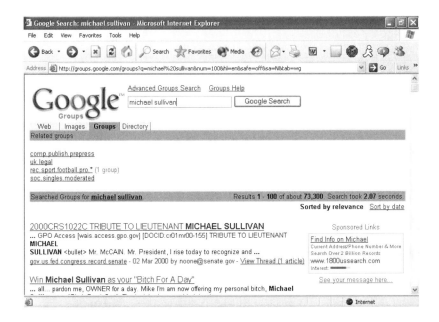

By using

+Michael+Sullivan+Naperville+Police

I get back twenty hits.

And finally, using

"Michael Sullivan"+Naperville+Police"

I get back no matches.

As you can see, there are many different areas and ways to search for information.

I recommend searching for information on a regular basis. I know I search about twice a month because I use this exercise when teaching classes.

The most devastating piece of personal information, for most people, is not their name, but a number. Specifically, your Social Security number. Try searching for your Social Security number, then your telephone number, and finally your address. Again, do not overreact if you get information back. Read the articles and see what they say. I know in classes teaching police officers we have found articles on the officers. It's not really that surprising since a lot of their work is covered by the news media and their names may appear in the stories. Also many have been involved in court proceedings that have become public records.

How does your personal information become public record? Easy. An article that talks about your daughter's accomplishments appears, then lists your home phone number, and finally links to a map showing where you live and offering driving directions to your home. A warranty card for a company that sells its database. A contest entry. Any or all of these can cause your information to become public.

If you find your Social Security number online, I would suggest one of the first things you should do is run a credit check on yourself. Talk to your local bank or credit union to see if there has been any unauthorized activity on your credit. Did anyone use your information in an attempt to get a credit card or loan?

▶ 1.5 Graphic child pornography sent via e-mail

*This should be reported to authorities, but it requires special handling. You **must not** print out this material, especially the images.*

If you receive graphic child pornography here are your options:

1. Report spam immediately to your ISP so they can block the offending spammer.

2. Notify your local law enforcement and follow their suggestions for how to follow up on the complaint.

3. Send the complaint to the National Center for Missing and Exploited Children and they will get the material into the hands of the proper authority.

4. Contact one of the Internet Crimes Against Children Units (ICAC) working in conjunction with the FBI's Operation Innocent Images.

5. Contact your state police for information on the ICAC unit nearest you. Again, I cannot stress how important it is that you not reproduce anything from these sites, even the best of intentions can cause problems.

6. *Remember* the best defense against viewing harassing or destructive attachments is not to open any e-mail from a sender you do not recognize. In fact, the e-mail settings for America Online will help you with this safety feature. You can tell the system to only accept the e-mail from trusted names; any others will be rejected before you ever get the chance to accidentally click on them. This is a very good way to set up your child's e-mail account.

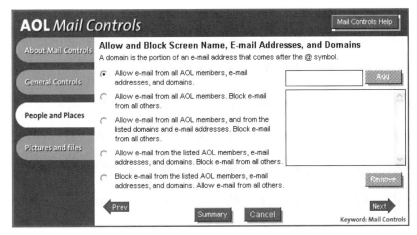

7. Make sure your virus protection is up to date. Most people download their virus protection and then forget about it. McAfee.com has a program called Virus Scan Online.

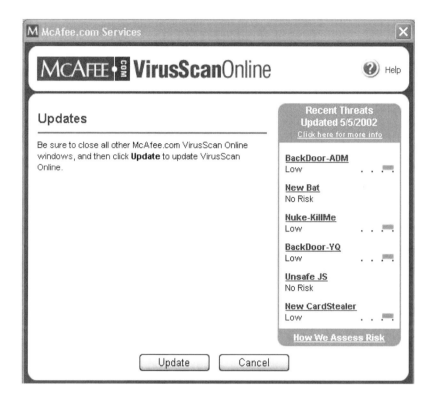

The virus software sits on the taskbar as you go about your business. Whenever there is an outbreak of a new virus, the program automatically notifies you that an update to the virus identification library is needed.

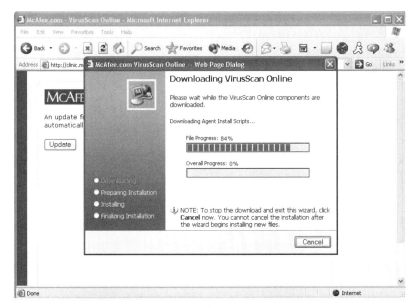

You just click on the notification window and within a minute the software runs back to its home site, gets the needed updates, brings them back and installs them on your computer, and then closes down until the next update is needed.

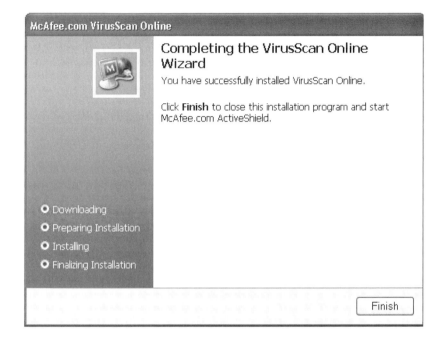

Talk about piece of mind, this is fantastic; I do love automation when it works.

▶ 1.6 Contact from Online Predators

Because of the limited amount of resources available to law enforcement, we must prioritize which threat takes precedent. There are only so many trained officers to investigate crimes committed via the computer. Those officers must prioritize what cases come first, and that means any case with the possibility of immediate danger or harm to a child will have priority over, say, persistent spam from an online pornographer.

The online predator is the highest on the priority chart

and has to be dealt with. This is where most of law enforcement's resources are being spent. In this chapter we will look at all of these examples, especially focusing on the traveler, or the online predator. We will look at the grooming techniques that online predators use to gain the trust of your child and their ability to manipulate your child for their purposes.

Before we can protect our children from predators we have to know how they gain access to our children.

2 Online Predators: Who They Are and How They Work

There are traditional predators and online predators, and they are surprisingly different types of people. Nevertheless, they are both extremely dangerous, and the number of online predators is rapidly growing.

▶ 2.1 The traditional predator

First, let's get to know the online predator's predecessor, the traditional child predator.

By the way, you have already noticed that we call them *predators* or *travelers*. We also use technical police jargon in the office such as "offender," "bad guy," and "maggot." A sense of humor is probably the most needed asset when you are working in this area of law enforcement.

In the police force, we usually avoid medical terminology like "pedophile" to describe traditional or online predators.

We are not medical professionals and are not qualified to offer an opinion on the particular sickness that afflicts them. We feel our terminology is accurate and easier to defend if used on the witness stand in court.

Pedophilia is a medical term. It refers to sexual thoughts and behaviors focused on a child, generally age thirteen or younger.

This is the term you hear used quite often when stories are written about predators on the Internet. However it is not accurate for most of the subjects we deal with during most of the online investigations.

The more accurate term is *preferential child molester/child pornographer*. This is a person who gets sexual gratification from actual physical contact with children and from fantasies he has while viewing children engaged in sexual activity or in sexually suggestive poses.

This is the one engaged in:

1. trading of child pornography on the Internet.
2. graphic sexual conversations with children.
3. grooming or luring children from the safety of their homes.
4. traveling across cities, states, and countries to engage in sexual activities with children.

It is from this type of behavior the police term *traveler* was created.

The traditional child predator:

1. is male.
2. is age 18–35.
3. suffers from a sense of low self-esteem.

4. has very little experience with women.
5. feels a sense of inadequacy.
6. thinks no one cares about him.
7. feels socially incompetent.
8. believes others will reject him.

▶ 2.2 The online predator

Now let's look at the online predator. Most people assume that traditional predators and online predators are one and the same. The online predator:

1. is male.
2. is age 30–65.
3. has a successful career (middle to upper management).
4. has an upper middle class or above lifestyle.
5. is a college graduate (not unusual to have post graduate degree).
6. was married at one time or is currently married.
7. has children of his own that are older then the children he is grooming or molesting.

Immediately it becomes clear that these two groups are entirely different sections of society. The reasons are not hard to understand.

First, the online predator has to have the money or a job that permits him access to costly products and services such as a computer, an online service, and peripheral devices such as scanners, CD burners, Web cameras, and digital cameras.

In most cases, the predator's employer is providing the Internet access, laptop computer, and e-mail. The technology is necessary for the offender to do his job, keep in touch with the office when he travels, or maintain productivity when on the road or selling via the Internet.

What begins as productivity can lead to crime. Time that may have been spent drinking at a hotel bar can now be spent online.

The Internet predator finds Web sites to visit, enters chat rooms, and finally engages in private conversations with children.

The fact that they have access to technology and are trusted by their companies tells us something else about these Internet predators. They are, to an extent, successful men in business, and are often supervisors. Most attended college in preparation for their careers and, in some cases, have continued with their academic training and have gone on to post-graduate degrees.

These offenders would never have thought of going to a park or playground to gain access to a child. They are men armed with plenty of technology and an understanding that the Internet makes them anonymous. They typically began their careers before computers became a fact of business life, and well before the common use of the Internet. They often are as unsure of themselves with technology as the ordinary parent.

However, for the vast majority of these types of offenders the Internet is *not* an anonymous forum. Most of them make it very easy to track and identify predators if the investigator has the necessary tools and training.

If online predators knew how easily we track them once we find their trail, there would be a lot fewer of them out there. In fact, one of the motivations to write this book is not only to help parents protect their children, but to scare potential online predators into thinking before they commit crimes. The anonymity they want to have is simply not available to someone of their limited technical skills. It takes more than a dial-up and some fancy equipment to hide from trained investigators. And it turns out that offenders know less about the technology then trained law enforcement does.

This is a surprise. But it shouldn't be.

Predators are not highly-trained hackers, and law enforcement has seen major advances in technology and training. There are outstanding units within the Federal Bureau of Investigation, Customs, Postal Inspectors, Secret Service, and individual local law enforcement agencies around the country that are well-qualified for this type of work—departments such as the San Jose and Redondo Beach Police Departments in California, the Medford Police Department in Massachusetts, the Hillsbourgh Sheriff's Department in the Tampa Bay, Florida, area, the United States Army Military Police Training at Fort Leonard Wood, Missouri, and the Champaign County Sheriffs Department, the Illinois Attorney General's Office, and, of course, the Naperville Police Department in Illinois, just to name a few.

They have some of the most capable technologically trained police officers in the world. They have forged partnerships with private corporations in the technology industry, which allows them access to some of the brightest minds in the field.

So why is there a problem? The truth is that for the average untrained law enforcement official, computer technology and Internet predators are as intimidating to them as they are to the average parent.

▶ 2.3 Why are there more predators now than there were before?

The advantage they have is in their numbers. There are so many predators appearing on the Internet that law enforcement does not have the resources to track down every one. Current estimates gauge online users at approximately 540 million users worldwide. If only one person in ten thousand is an online predator (the equivalent of having only forty online predators in the city of Cleveland), that leaves fifty-four thousand predators online. Now you can start to see the battle law enforcement has in front of itself.

▶ 2.4 Protecting ourselves: first steps

Our best protection lies in community education.

Community presentations, books, and shows like *Oprah* that describe the grooming techniques, the offenders being arrested, and the legal ramifications, can protect thousands more children in one shot then law enforcement can with all the undercover stings and arrests we can make.

Education needs to be a part of every community, although victims today are typically suburban, middle-class children, more and more children will be at risk as the cost of technology drops. Children in the inner city normally do not have the same unmonitored access to a computer and online service that children in suburban areas do. In the future, more and more children in more and more communities will be at risk.

Although online predators may not be the most sophisticated people in the world, they are relentless. Some of the predators I have worked on arresting have shocked me at the extent to which they were willing to go to get to their victims.

There was the fifty-year-old sex offender who drove eighteen hours through a blinding snowstorm to get to the location where he could molest a young boy.

Then there was the convicted sex offender, imprisoned for molesting children, who celebrated his release by attempting to abduct a child from a playground, and was sent straight back to prison. He celebrated his second release by finding a new career on the Internet—collecting and distributing child pornography. He is back in prison again, and we hope this is his last attempt at harming children and his final sentence.

Offenders have admitted, after traveling across the state, the country, or from other countries, that using the Internet was not their first attempt at molesting children. In one case, the subject had spent the summer driving around his small town stalking children on the playground, at the local swimming pool, and convenience store.

2.4.1 Where the traditional predator lurks, operates, and gains the trust of your child

School grounds and parks are the traditional predator's hunting grounds.

He uses:

1. toys.
2. remote controlled cars or boats.
3. fancy kites.
4. inventive come on lines such as "your mother and father sent me to get you," or "I have lost my dog and need help finding it" (even going so far as to carry a leash and collar).

The down side to this method is that traditional predators can be seen. Seen by other children, parents in the park watching other children, the people who live by the park, teachers or teacher's aides on the school grounds, and even the passing police patrol car.

For this reason, many predators choose to operate a special kind of house instead of cruising in public for the child. The house in the neighborhood where children know they can go for unsupervised activities, maybe unlimited video games, alcohol, or other drugs. All free at the beginning but then over a period of time the true cost of these things is learned.

The path to evil is always the most carefully paved.

First, there are pictures shown to the child. Later, the predator shows nude images, often of other children appearing to enjoy sexual contact with predators, to de-sensitize the child. Then sexual contact comes, and, finally, documentation of the sexual activity in pictures and movies.

These are activities the children are too embarrassed to admit to parents and even friends. Often, the further children are unwittingly led down the path to abuse, the more reluctant they become to talk about it.

▶ 2.5 How the online predator lurks, operates and gains the trust of your child

The online predator has the virtual playground, a playground that allows him the power to "watch" children without anyone knowing he is in the playground, or what child he is attempting to lure away.

With the computer and an online service, the predator can surf for his personal preference—boys, girls, different nationalities, different ages—until he finds the one he wants.

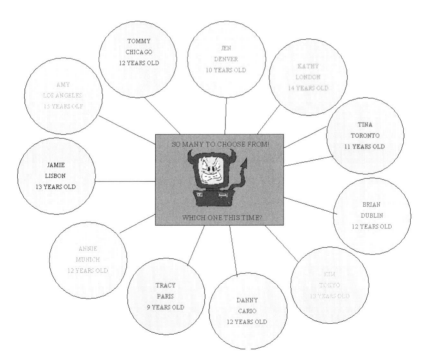

The virtual playground has provided the predator with the ability to sit in the privacy of his own home, office, or hotel on the road and use search engines to locate his victim.

The predator may gain information about his next victim from a list of his favorite Web sites or newsgroups. These are Web sites and newsgroups catering to pornography or child pornography, and are as specific as "pedophilia," "boys nude," or "preteen rape."

These sites do exist and are even promoted on the Internet. Here's something scarier. Most of them are legal.

How can that be? Well, the machine housing the Web site, newsgroup, and the images of child pornography can be based in countries which do not have laws against these activities. As long as the images remain on that machine in another country there are no laws being broken here and we have no authority to shut down the machine.

However, what does happen here in the United States that *is* illegal is accessing the site and downloading images. The online predator downloads images for his own satisfaction, to trade with other predators, and to use the images to show to a potential victim. The images are used to prove to the child that sexual contact between children and adults is acceptable.

"See? The children in the pictures are doing what I told you to do. They're smiling. They're having fun. Don't you want to have fun?"

Once those images have been downloaded, we have a violation of the law and law enforcement can take action. You as a parent can expect someone to do something about it!

2.5.1 Online predator chat rooms

```
#0!!!!!!!!!!!!!!11yr3
#0!!!!!!!!!!!!!!12yr76
#0!!!!!!!!!!!!!!17yr67
#0!!!!!!!!!!!!!!18yr13
#0!!!!!!!!!!!!!!21yr28
#0!!!!!!!!!!!!!!pret12
#0!!!!!!!!!!!!!!pret36
#0!!!!!!!!!!!!!!16yrd50
#0!!!!!!!!!!!!!!ALLSE3
#0!!!!!!!!!!!!!prete53
#0!!!!!!!!!!!!!prete67
#0!!!!!!!!!!!!!cheer13
#0!!!!!!!!!!!!!little10
#0!!!!!!!!!!!!!pedop15
```

Most of the rooms listed above are chat rooms specializing in pornography and child abuse. Starting from the top and working down the room name and topic of the room is:

- 11-year-old sex—trading sex pictures of young children
- 12-year-old sex—sexual role playing room
- 17-year-old sex—trading sex pictures
- 18-year-old sex—trading sex pictures
- 21-year-old sex—trading sex pictures
- Preteen002—best preteen sex pictures and videos
- Preteen101—best preteen sex pictures and videos
- 16-year-old sex—teen sex pictures
- all sex pics—sex picture trading
- Preteen00—best sex pictures and videos
- Preteen666—best sex pictures and videos

These are actual online chat rooms. They're sick. They're disturbing. But there is protection available. Your child can be safe from these rooms using straightforward software and common sense.

▶ 2.6 The online predator and your child's online profile—the predator's spyglass

Filling out a profile can be the single most important thing you do with your children when setting up their Internet service provider accounts.

Profiles can contain tons of valuable information for a predator. Examples include name, hometown, gender, and birthdate. With this information, the predator can seek out victims easily. A simple query to the ISP's database will do the trick.

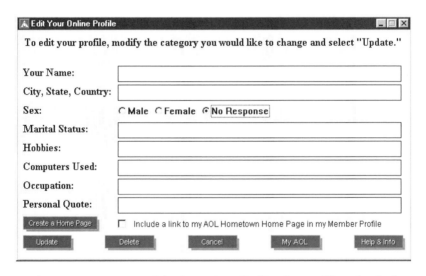

As you can see, with America Online's profile, the information has been curtailed, not allowing boxes for age or the name of your school. In other ISP formats, the information is not as protected and children enter personal information such as age, home address, and even telephone numbers.

The predator reads the information in the profile to

begin the stalking process. He obtains the victim's name, birthdate, and hobbies.

If the victim entered in the optional information, the predator learns what school the child attends, what places the child frequents, and if he or she is having trouble at school or with his or her parents.

If the child has indicated his or her school and a sport he or she has played (perhaps even his or her jersey number) the predator may contact the school, order a yearbook, and have a school picture of the child.

The guideline for filling out a profile is to *keep it short*. If you're going to use your real name, just put in your first name, never your last name.

For example, if your first name is Michael, then enter Mike, or if you have a nickname such as Sully, then enter Sully and nothing more.

Never ever put in your birthdate, home telephone number, or home address.

▶ 2.7 The online predator and the chat room—the predator's hunting ground

If you have never been in a chat room and wonder what they are all about, let me explain that not all chat rooms are created equal.

Chat rooms are an offshoot of electronic bulletin boards, which are offshoots of traditional bulletin boards. At first, people posted messages, ads, and queries. When the bulletin boards went electronic, you could post *responses* to a *post-*

ing. In chat rooms, postings and responses can be done in real time.

All chat rooms share one characteristic. They are areas of the Internet where you can exchange messages with a large number of people at one time, and where there is the option to join a group *chat* where everyone in the chat room can view every comment.

Some ISPs such as AOL provide their own *chat rooms* or you can use programs such as MIRC or ICQ to access chat areas. Chat rooms can be general, or limited to a specific interest (e.g. romance or horse racing).

Among chat rooms there are moderated rooms and un-moderated rooms. Here's what that means:

2.7.1 Moderated chat rooms

In a moderated chat room, a person monitors what is being said in the chat room to make sure the comments are appropriate for that chat room.

Say this is a chat room about gardening. The moderator would discourage people from chatting about rebuilt antique cars. The moderator would also monitor the language used in the chat room. Anyone using profanity is warned, or kicked out and banned from any further participation in that chat room. Also, the moderator monitors any personal attacks, crude, deliberately mean or vicious comments directed towards members of the chat room. These are known as *flames* or, when people begin to exchange flames, as *flame wars.*

2.7.2 Un-moderated chat rooms

In an un-moderated chat room no one really monitors what is said, or what type of language is used. These are rooms that are set up and designed to chat on a specific topic (e.g. ChicagoBurbs for chat with people from or about the Chicago suburbs). It can also be used to bring people together from that area to chat and possibly meet in real life after establishing a friendship online. A meeting of this type should never be entered into lightly. That goes for us adults as well as children. Do not forget the person on the other end of the computer is a stranger!

1. No matter how much you chat with that person, you do not really know who he or she is, what he or she looks like, or what his or her background is like. Never allow children to meet anyone from the Internet—and I mean *anyone*—without your permission and without your accompaniment.

2. Make sure the person your child is meeting knows that his or her parents are coming along.

3. Make the meeting at a public place, such as a restaurant or mall, where you can meet and get to know each other without giving away where either of you live.

4. If you go to the meeting and the twelve-year-old boy you were going to meet turns out to be a fifty-year-old man, you now have learned a very valuable lesson and done so safely.

5. This rule *applies to adults also*. Never meet anyone you met on the Internet alone. Take a friend with you.

Again, make the meeting in a public place and don't be surprised when the person you meet in real life does not turn out to be the one described on the Internet.

For those of you who have never seen a chat room, this is what one looks like.

This is the chat room CyberAngels on Internet Relay Chat (IRC). This is a group of individuals who volunteer to keep the chat room open and help other users with questions about IRC chat and proper online behavior.

As you can see, getting used to chatting takes a bit of time. The first thing you notice is everyone is talking at the same time.

The chat scrolls by and you have to follow the lines of chat that are relevant to your conversation. In some chat rooms there can be hundreds of different conversations going on simultaneously, or everyone in the chat room my be involved in just one topic.

There can be any number of people in a chat room. For example, there can be one hundred people in an IRC chat room. Some AOL Live! chats that feature live interaction with celebrities can involve thousands of visitors in one giant room. In other chat room formats on other service providers, they may limit the number of people in any one chat room. AOL allows twenty-three people in a standard chat room. If anyone else wants to join, someone must leave the room or the twenty-fourth person can start a similarly-named room and have twenty-two more people join him or her in the new chat room.

When in a chat room, whatever you say will be seen by everyone in that room.

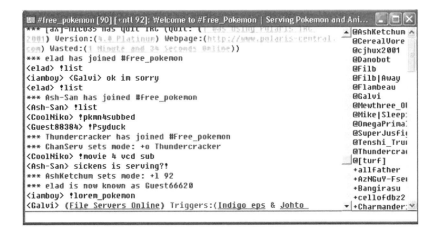

In this chat room about Pokemon, on the right you can see the list of all the people currently in the room.

Chatting in the room itself is not the preferred method of a predator. Predators use chat rooms as a hunting ground to locate their victim. They look at what is being said. Is there a child of the sex and age they are looking for in the chat room? Is that child having a good time online, are others chatting with the child, or are the other members of the chat room picking on the child?

If the child is being ignored, what topic is the child trying to discuss? The predator checks the child's profile to gain further intelligence information about how to approach the child. If there is sufficient information, the predator has an opening to begin a conversation with the child. The conversation most likely will not begin in a chat room, but in a private conversation.

▶ 2.8 The online predator makes his approach with a private message

No matter what Internet service provider you select, there probably will be some form of chat room available to your child. Even if the ISP does not supply a chat room there are many Web-based chat rooms that your child can enter free of charge. Most children can show any parent how easy it is to find the chat rooms.

Once in a chat room, and after finding a friend to chat with, your child will probably find his or her way to a more private form of chatting. This private form of chat has many different names, depending on what ISP or chat program you are using. Some of the more common names used are private message, instant message, and instant messenger.

For most, the names are interchangeable and are basically used to signify a private conversation, even if you are using a particular format but use the generic term of messaging.

▶ 2.9 The key questions that predators ask children—and why

Now the predator is ready to approach the child.

Watch in the example below how the predator structures his questions in a way to gain more and more personal information from the child without the child realizing what information is being given away. The questions asked by Tommy are questions I have seen repeatedly over the years in the hundreds of online investigations in which I have been involved.

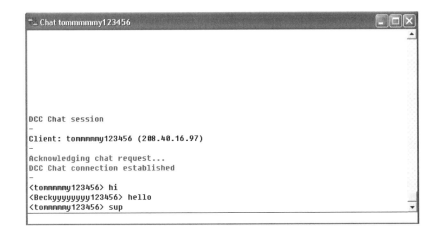

Sup?

In the private message Tommy has said hello to Becky and asked "sup"—that's chat short hand for "what's up?" After Becky replied, Tommy continued to ask questions about Becky.

Chatting has given birth to an entirely new language. When typing, words that can be shortened down to a single letter or two are used instead of typing the entire word. During conversations, you are likely to see the letter "r" used for the word "are." "R U" means "are you" and so on. Typed symbols known as emoticons add smiles :-), winks ;-), and frowns :-(to the vocabulary. Abbreviations such as LOL for laughing out loud or ROFL for rolling on the floor laughing are other examples of this chat room language.

For a full listing of these emoticons try using the search

engine Google (*www.google.com*) and type in the word emoticons. You will receive links to numerous sites that have pages and pages of the emoticons displayed and explained.

A,S,L?

In our sample chat, Tommy asked three more questions with just the use of three letters: a, s, l. This is chat shorthand for asking for your age, gender or sex, and the location where you live.

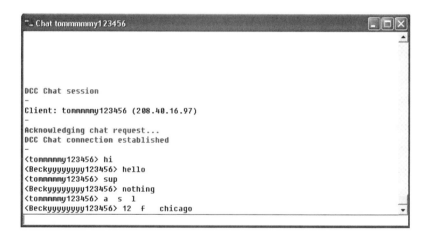

Becky has responded that she is twelve, female, and that she lives in Chicago. These three questions are very common in chat and private messaging. *The proper answer would be no answer at all*, or to give a minimal response such as "a girl in high school" with no indication of location or true age. If this is a predator and not another junior high school student, it will start to dissuade the predator from talking to this child. In our Internet safety program, I usually only need six questions to isolate one student from the forty to ninety students attending the program. The children are able to see for themselves just how quickly they can be located.

Tommy has continued to ask questions that would help him locate the specific geographical area of Chicago where Becky lives. He related that he lived in the Chicago area also and is trying to find landmarks to help him pinpoint Becky's home.

By naming more and more of the landmarks, Tommy will eventually know the area for Becky's home and would be able to go to the area to look for her.

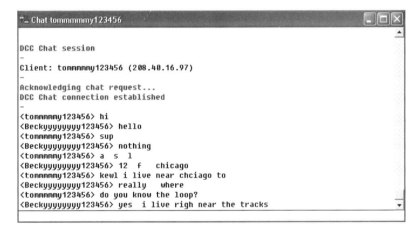

The next sets of questions are ones that should sound the alarm bells. Whenever your child is asked any of the following questions he or she should notify you immediately.

Do you have any brothers or sisters?

The question seems innocent enough. If your child has siblings, the predator may chat about what a pain it is to have a little brother or an older sister. He will type something in

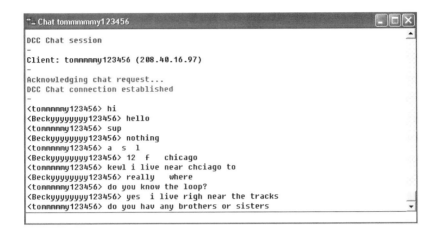

```
Chat tommmmmy123456                                    _ □ X

DCC Chat session
-
Client: tommmmmy123456 (208.40.16.97)
-
Acknowledging chat request...
DCC Chat connection established
-
<tommmmmy123456> hi
<Beckyyyyyyyy123456> hello
<tommmmmy123456> sup
<Beckyyyyyyyy123456> nothing
<tommmmmy123456> a  s  l
<Beckyyyyyyyy123456> 12  f   chicago
<tommmmmy123456> kewl i live near chciago to
<Beckyyyyyyyy123456> really   where
<tommmmmy123456> do you know the loop?
<Beckyyyyyyyy123456> yes  i live righ near the tracks
<tommmmmy123456> do you hav any brothers or sisters
```

order to soothe and distract your child from his real intent. The predator is actually starting to assess the threat level: *How likely is it that he will be caught talking to this child?*

Who uses your computer?

If the child is the only one using the computer, the parents are computer illiterate, and there are no siblings, the predator begins to believe that the threat to him is low.

```
Chat tommmmmy123456                                    _ □ X

Client: tommmmmy123456 (208.40.16.97)
-
Acknowledging chat request...
DCC Chat connection established
-
<tommmmmy123456> hi
<Beckyyyyyyyy123456> hello
<tommmmmy123456> sup
<Beckyyyyyyyy123456> nothing
<tommmmmy123456> a  s  l
<Beckyyyyyyyy123456> 12  f   chicago
<tommmmmy123456> kewl i live near chciago to
<Beckyyyyyyyy123456> really   where
<tommmmmy123456> do you know the loop?
<Beckyyyyyyyy123456> yes  i live righ near the tracks
<tommmmmy123456> do you hav any brothers or sisters
<Beckyyyyyyyy123456> no
<tommmmmy123456> who uses your computer
```

Where is your computer?

Does anyone really care where you have your computer? Not really. They just care that you have one so you can chat with them and be online friends. However, for the predator, the location of the computer is extremely important. The answer a predator hopes to hear is that the computer is in the child's room or in the basement, anywhere it is out of sight of the parents, and the likelihood of anyone seeing what is said on the screen is remote.

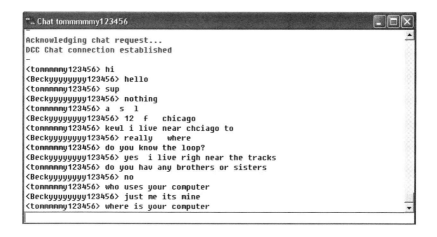

```
Chat tommmmmy123456                                    _ □ ×

Acknowledging chat request...
DCC Chat connection established
—
<tommmmmy123456> hi
<Beckyyyyyyyy123456> hello
<tommmmmy123456> sup
<Beckyyyyyyyy123456> nothing
<tommmmmy123456> a  s  l
<Beckyyyyyyyy123456> 12  f   chicago
<tommmmmy123456> kewl i live near chciago to
<Beckyyyyyyyy123456> really   where
<tommmmmy123456> do you know the loop?
<Beckyyyyyyyy123456> yes  i live righ near the tracks
<tommmmmy123456> do you hav any brothers or sisters
<Beckyyyyyyyy123456> no
<tommmmmy123456> who uses your computer
<Beckyyyyyyyy123456> just me its mine
<tommmmmy123456> where is your computer
```

Are you alone?

The question *"Are you alone?"* has never been asked without the conversation turning in a bad direction or to sexually related topics in the next few minutes. This is one question you want set in any software you have in use protecting your children. In a later chapter I will talk about software that will notify you immediately if someone ever asks this question of your child.

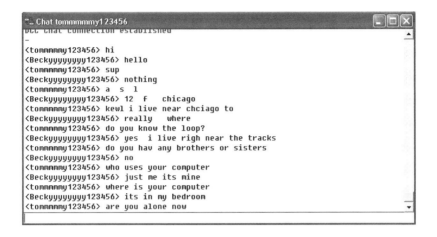

```
■_ Chat tommmmmy123456                                    ▢▢✕
DCC Chat Connection Established
_
<tommmmy123456> hi
<Beckyyyyyyyy123456> hello
<tommmmy123456> sup
<Beckyyyyyyyy123456> nothing
<tommmmy123456> a  s  l
<Beckyyyyyyyy123456> 12  f   chicago
<tommmmy123456> kewl i live near chciago to
<Beckyyyyyyyy123456> really   where
<tommmmy123456> do you know the loop?
<Beckyyyyyyyy123456> yes  i live righ near the tracks
<tommmmy123456> do you hav any brothers or sisters
<Beckyyyyyyyy123456> no
<tommmmy123456> who uses your computer
<Beckyyyyyyyy123456> just me its mine
<tommmmy123456> where is your computer
<Beckyyyyyyyy123456> its in my bedroom
<tommmmy123456> are you alone now
```

What school do you go to?

The predator finds the child by asking questions such as: "What school do you go to?" and "Do you play sports?"

Remember not all predators will be this subtle. In one case I worked I had the undercover profile of a small boy online. I received a message saying "Hey do you want to F**k?"

```
■_ Chat tommmmmy123456                                    ▢▢✕
<tommmmy123456> hi
<Beckyyyyyyyy123456> hello
<tommmmy123456> sup
<Beckyyyyyyyy123456> nothing
<tommmmy123456> a  s  l
<Beckyyyyyyyy123456> 12  f   chicago
<tommmmy123456> kewl i live near chciago to
<Beckyyyyyyyy123456> really   where
<tommmmy123456> do you know the loop?
<Beckyyyyyyyy123456> yes  i live righ near the tracks
<tommmmy123456> do you hav any brothers or sisters
<Beckyyyyyyyy123456> no
<tommmmy123456> who uses your computer
<Beckyyyyyyyy123456> just me its mine
<tommmmy123456> where is your computer
<Beckyyyyyyyy123456> its in my bedroom
<tommmmy123456> are you alone now
<Beckyyyyyyyy123456> yes
<tommmmy123456> what school do you go to
```

That was how the predator said hello.

What followed was an explanation that the subject was a forty-something businessman who flew around the country. When he landed, he got online and looked for all the young boys online in the area where he was staying. He then asked the boys if they wanted to meet up for sex. He asked if I was interested.

It just so happened my team members and I were ready to meet him. He plead guilty to the charge of sexual solicitation of a minor.

▶ 2.10 How the online predator uses an address

Armed with all of his newly acquired information, the predator turns on his computer, locates the Web page for St. Michelle's in Chicago (don't bother looking it up, its not a real school). He looks for the soccer team page. There's a schedule of the upcoming games, which means he can go to the game and find number 9 for St. Michelle's.

If the school puts up pictures of the teams on the Web site the predator can just bring up the picture and look for number 9, he does not even have to attend a game to get a picture of the child. He now knows exactly to whom he is chatting and what she looks like.

It's a dangerous world.

What can you do? First, install and use the protection software, and always, always, always talk to your children.

▶ 2.11 How the online predator uses a phone number

In a later chapter we will cover the setup and use of the software, but now, let me demonstrate what the predator could do with your home phone number.

"Tommy" has convinced Becky that they could be friends and that they may even already hang out at the same arcade. So it seems natural to Becky to agree to meet at the arcade and play some video games together. It doesn't seem dangerous to Becky because "Tommy" has convinced her of his identity and she meets friends at the arcade all the time.

In this context, giving "Tommy" her home telephone number does not seem like such a dangerous thing to do. However, once "Tommy" has the number he uses one of the oldest and simplest tools available on the Internet. He accesses reverse white pages.

There are over one hundred reverse white pages sites on the Internet, and they are opposite of the white pages of a phone book that we use all the time. "Tommy" will not be starting with a name and looking up a number.

```
Chat tommmmmy123456                                    _ □ X
<tommmmmy123456> who uses your computer
<Beckyyyyyyyy123456> just me its mine
<tommmmmy123456> where is your computer
<Beckyyyyyyyy123456> its in my bedroom
<tommmmmy123456> are you alone now
<Beckyyyyyyyy123456> yes
<tommmmmy123456> what school do you go to
<Beckyyyyyyyy123456> St. Michelles
<tommmmmy123456> do you play any sports
<Beckyyyyyyyy123456> soccer
<tommmmmy123456> cool did you get to pick your number
<Beckyyyyyyyy123456> yes  i got number 9  my favorite one
<tommmmmy123456> do you ever go to the arcade on 10th street
<Beckyyyyyyyy123456> yes all the time its only two blocks from my house
<tommmmmy123456> me to    maybe we could meet there some time
<Beckyyyyyyyy123456> but how would i know when to meet you there
<tommmmmy123456> you could give me your telephone number and i could call you
  and we could pick a time to meet
<Beckyyyyyyyy123456> oh   ok my phone number is 630 420 6666
```

He will start with a number and look up your name and address.

First, he found that the telephone number (630) 420-6666 registers to

Naperville City Of, Public Utilities Dept Of, (630) 420-6666,
Naperville, IL 60540

Next he was able to get a map showing where Becky lives.

Then he got an aerial view of the address.

DIRECTIONS	DISTANCE
1: Start out going East on WILLIAMS ST towards S COUNTY FARM RD by turning right.	0.01 miles
2: Turn RIGHT onto S COUNTY FARM RD.	0.12 miles
3: Turn RIGHT onto IL-38.	0.94 miles
4: Turn LEFT onto WINFIELD RD.	1.99 miles
5: Turn RIGHT onto BUTTERFIELD RD.	2.01 miles
6: Turn LEFT onto IL-59.	4.03 miles
7: Turn LEFT onto AURORA AVE.	1.47 miles
Total Estimated Time: **18 minutes**	**Total Distance:** **10.57 miles**

And finally, he was able to obtain driving directions from his residence to Becky's house.

Since 1994, all the cases I have worked on involving a predator and chatting have been done by a private message, instant message, instant messenger, or some type of private communications program. This is why private chat puts your children at grave risk. With a little communication between you and your children, you can prepare them to behave properly if they are confronted by this type of predator.

▶ 2.12 What could Becky and her parents have done better?

1. Spent more time with Becky teaching her the rules of the road when it comes to chatting online. If she is going to chat, she can NEVER give out her phone number, her full name, or her school.

2. Installed and used software that helps detect when "Tommy," the predator, is online and trying to manipulate your trusting child.

▶ 2.13 Video conferencing

Video conferencing is an up-and-coming area of concern for parents and law enforcement alike.

What is a videoconference? It's a combination of two video cameras and two microphones used so that people can see each other as they chat. Today, cameras are also integrated with computers so that you can see with whom you are chatting online. These cameras are called Web cams.

However, the predator of today uses the camera to expose himself to unsuspecting children. He uses the videoconference as his own private street corner on the Information Superhighway.

This is a high-tech, twenty-first century version of the pervert exhibitionist, the flasher we used to arrest in public libraries and in schoolyards and on street corners. He sits in his chair, connected to the whole world via the Internet, advertises himself as a middle-aged man looking for nice clean chat, and waits for the next victim to surf on into his web.

▶ 2.14 How the predator lures the child into a videoconference

In this example, the predator is a middle-aged male and Tina is a thirteen-year-old girl. The predator has lured her into an online conversation. The predator has video conferencing in mind. He knows that the software is free, and it is easy enough to install that Tina can do it herself. The predator asks if she has a Web camera. She doesn't. He purchases one for $15 and mails it to her.

The predator will then instruct Tina how to install the software, invite her into a videoconference session, and proceed to masturbate in front of her.

It happens more than you think.

The predator will go a step further. He will ask Tina to perform a sex act on camera. He will ask her to undress during the video conferencing session, and then masturbate. The predator will not only watch her. He will record the entire session. He will enter the chat rooms we covered earlier, to trade images or videos of Tina with other predators.

Before long, Tina's video is traded thousands of times and travels around the world. Predators who have nothing more in mind than their own gratification exploit her in countries she will never visit, in cities she will never know.

This is a newer version of mailing cameras that instantly develop photographs of children, so that they can take nude photographs of themselves and mail them to the predators.

3 How Does It Begin? How Do We Stop Predators?

It all starts with a simple, apparently harmless visit to a chat room. The good news? Using software to protect your child in chat rooms can help. But also follow these three rules.

▶ 3.1 The Three Nevers of Online Child Protection

1. **Never forget that you are not alone—there is help available from law enforcement, and resources like this book.**

   Ask your local law enforcement agency if they have any information on children and the Internet. Check with your local school and find out how they are protecting your child's identity and what information is available from the school Web site. (In the resource section of this book you will find other helpful sites with additional information on protecting your child.)

2. **Never give out personal information or discuss personal subjects with a stranger online.**

   When it comes to filling out an online profile, use only a first name or nickname, nothing more. Never give out, or permit your child to give out, a last name, address, phone number, or school name. Never discuss personal topics with anyone unless you know them personally from school, extra curricular activates, or a sports team.

3. **Never overreact if your child tells you about a problem with an online experience.**

   Never criticize your child's judgment. Remain calm and remember the fact that your child is coming to you for assistance. Remember that your child has been tricked by a crafty predator, or perhaps has simply made a mistake and clicked on an inappropriate link. Nothing that happens online should prevent you and your children from communicating with each other about safety.

▶ 3.2 Notification of authorities

The rule of thumb on notifying the authorities is to let them know when you receive any illegal item, harassment, or a death threat.

Make sure you report any illegal activity to your local police department. The fact is that the average online home has more and newer computer equipment then the average law enforcement agency. The citizens of any given town or city spends more time online than the law enforcement agency can.

However, when doing this, be careful not to violate the law yourself. Especially when dealing with sites advertising child pornography. Downloading child pornography, even with the best of intentions, is illegal.

The mere possession of child pornography is a felony in most countries and in most states in the United States. Save the Web address for the site doing the advertising and send that address to the police. Let the police go to the site and check the images.

One thing to keep in mind is that a large number of sites on the Internet advertise they have the "youngest teens" on the Internet. However, after receiving hundreds of complaints about sites like these, I have learned that most of them are lying about the *teen* part. In checking the sites I have found that most of the girls are clearly in their mid-twenties to mid-thirties. The advertisement is nothing more then a come-on to get you to buy a membership.

As for harassment and death threats, let me tell you about one case I worked on. I received a call from a deputy sheriff who related her niece, a high school student, was receiving death threats via e-mail.

The predator demanded nude images of the girl, or he would kill her. As the deadline for sending the images approached, the family began to take the threats more seriously and sent the niece to live with her aunt, a police officer, for safety. The aunt then contacted my unit at the Naperville police department and asked for assistance with the case.

It took just forty-five minutes to solve. First, we took the e-mail apart and were able to trace the origination of the e-mail to the girl's high school.

The sheriff visited the high school, met with the manager of information services, patched us in via a phone conference and within minutes we had pinpointed the exact machine used and had the name of a suspect.

The sheriff confronted the suspect, a teenage boy, and obtained a confession. The boy had no intention of carrying out the death threat. He simply wanted nude pictures of the girl.

We were not at all disappointed that it turned out to be nothing more than a high school prank. Firstly, we restored calm for the girl and her family. Secondly, I can speak, I think, for all policemen in saying we would rather run down thousands of false leads or nuisance complaints than to have someone be afraid they are being bothersome and not report the one case where a child is harmed.

▶ 3.3 Free speech and what you can expect from law enforcement

Free speech causes law enforcement the most problems with reports. If an online predator talks about his fantasy to harm a child, and he types it or says it and does not include any illegal pictures—and indicates that the text is for entertainment only—then law enforcement will find it to be almost impossible to prosecute this person.

The First Amendment, guaranteeing the right to free speech, covers the Internet also.

This does not mean that as law enforcement officials we would not be interested in knowing what members of our community are spreading these types of fantasies. However, understand that by the nature of the law there may not be a violation.

If those fantasies or actions are addressed to a specific individual, it may result in a prosecutable offense. It depends on the jurisdiction you live in, and your local law enforcement agency will be able to clarify this for you. The right to free speech is one of the most powerful rights we have. It is one that is well protected by our laws and government, but having such a right does not eliminate the need to use it responsibly.

PART TWO

Protecting Your Children ▶

2

Talking to Your Kids About the Internet

OVERVIEW

What You Will Learn

- How to take your children through a frank and comprehensive discussion about the Internet, including sample discussions.

How You Will Feel:

- Confident that your kids understand the family rules about the Internet, especially regarding safety

What Is Covered

- Reading up
- Prepping your stories
- Choosing the time and place
- Setting up the discussion
- Reviewing Internet terminology
- Relating your Internet stories
- Asking questions of your children
- Reinforcing after the discussion
- Making an online contract with your children

Detective Mike's Second Law

Nothing is more important in protecting your children than helping your children to protect themselves.

---

1 Prepping for the Discussion

▶ 1.1 Read up!

Before you start your chat with the kids, you'll want to read this book in its entirety, especially this chapter, and have it with you during the discussion.

Make a list of topics you will cover, if you feel more comfortable that way.

▶ 1.2 Prep your stories

During the discussion you will be using examples and stories to make the chat memorable and interesting. I have provided some generic stories and situations for you in the pages ahead, but your own stories will naturally be more interesting to your kids.

1. Did you ever have a scary or uncomfortable encounter with a stranger?
2. Did you ever meet someone over the Internet, telephone, or by mail that didn't turn out to be the person you thought he or she was?
3. Did you ever have an uncomfortable experience with a Web site, magazine, or TV show that promoted violence, sex, or drugs?
4. Did you ever click on one site and get numerous other sites opening, sites you never intended (or wanted) to see? This has happened to every Internet user without the proper software, and that includes your child. Explain that even Mom and Dad make mistakes and show how you reacted to the mistakes. Your child learns and copies behaviors from you.

Try to think of two examples. One, about something you encountered that made you uncomfortable. Two, about someone you encountered in life who did not turn out to be who you thought he or she was.

▶ 1.3 Choosing the time and place

Make sure that you have scheduled an uninterrupted evening in the privacy of your home and in a comfortable place where you can have lots of eye contact. The discussion will not take long, but it's better to have more time to fill than feel rushed by other commitments.

2 The Discussion

▶ 2.1. The set-up

1. Sometime in the early evening, tell your child, "I would like to have a discussion with you about safety and the Internet. No, you have not done anything wrong and you are not in trouble."

2. Make sure your child knows the discussion is open and friendly, not a punishment. I think we all understand the feeling that goes through us when we are told, "We need to talk." Nothing enjoyable ever followed those words. Avoid getting off on the wrong foot with your child.

3. Explain that as your child is growing older, there are more privileges to enjoy, and more responsibilities too. Responsibilities such as doing more chores around the house to get an allowance that allows them to have their own money. That as they grow older they are allowed to take driver's education and eventually drive a car, but along with the freedom of driving they have increased responsibilities. Driving

safely, the safety of the passengers in their car, and the care and maintenance of the car.

4. Explain that one of the privileges is access to the Internet. One of the responsibilities is to know and follow the family rules about the Internet.

5. Ask your child some questions.

> "What do you know about the Internet"?
>
> "What kind of people do we meet there?"
>
> "Why would we need to have a chat about safety and the Internet?"
>
> "Have you ever met a stranger online?"
>
> "Have you ever visited a Web site or read something online that made you feel uncomfortable?"

③ Reviewing the Terms

▶ **3.1**

It's a good idea to make sure your child knows the terms you will be using during the discussion. Also, you will want to make sure that *you* know the terms that your child will be using in answering some of your questions.

Don't be afraid during your discussion to let your children show you what they know about the computer and the Internet. As you discuss the different areas and content you should be just as prepared to learn from your children as much as you should be prepared to set the parameters of their computer use.

3.1.1 Picture/Movie

Any picture file, or movie file, or a file in the format *.pct, *.jpg, *.jpeg, or *.gif, *.avi, *.mpeg, *.mpg, *.rm, *.wmv.

3.1.2 Download

Any file transfer from the Internet to the home computer, such as sending an attached document or picture file, movie file, sound file, or text document.

3.1.3 Sounds/Music/Wav File

Any audio file that can be downloaded and played as if it were a sound on a cassette tape, CD, or, for us old folks, a record. Some of the content of the files can be highly inappropriate and violent. They are usually in the format of a *.wav, *.rm, or *.mp3.

3.1.4 File

The digital form of a document, picture, or Web page stored in your computer. File is the generic way of describing any type of information on your hard drive, whether it is a picture, text, movie, or song.

3.1.5 Screen name

Also known as user name or user ID, and associated with a password. Most Internet service providers allow you to use multiple screen names and these should be appropriate in nature. They should not be your child's full name, nor should they be suggestive or sexual in nature. Sleezey-Suzie12 would not be an appropriate screen name, yet I have seen several of this variety used by children. Sometimes children pick cute names not realizing the words have two meanings. Help your child choose their screen name, keep the name in a log with the appropriate password. Yes, you should know your child's password and he or she should understand that letting Mom and Dad have the password is part of being responsible for his or her actions. Responsible children don't need to hide their actions

3.1.6 Profile

The information that you store with your service provider when you sign up for your Internet service. Some or all of this information may be made available to other users of the service when they are online. Be careful when filling out the profile; follow the suggestions given to you in this book about entering personal information. Also, be careful to choose the information your child enters into the profile and make sure it is not a double entendre.

3.1.7 Chat room

The dedicated space of an online service where multiple users may exchange comments and dialogue in real time, simulating a free-for-all group conversation. This is like the old party line phone system where everyone hears what is being said.

3.1.8 Parental controls

Options given to parents and other primary account contacts regarding the access privileges given to their children. These controls include, but are not limited to, e-mail access, restriction from selected sites with graphic, sexual, or violent content, restriction in sending/receiving instant messages, and restrictions on viewing newsgroups or certain types of newsgroups. Be careful to check if the parental controls are all-encompassing. Do they only work when the browser is up and the ISP is connected? If this is the case, purchase additional software.

3.1.9 Screening/blocking

Software that permits the user to add parental controls such as denying access to questionable web sites as well as capturing information from questionable online encounters. Permitting parents to select the type of content that should not be viewed by their child, and using the software to filter out this type of content. Content such as inappropriate Web sites, violence, and the accidental release of personal information by your child.

3.1.10 Web cam/Video Conference

Camera located on top of a computer with online service permitting users to be shown by video while online. This can be the single most dangerous peripheral attached to your computer and should never be left in a child's room. See later chapters for how the camera can lead to trouble.

3.1.11 Instant Messages/Private Message/ Private Whisper/Instant Messenger

Known by a variety of nicknames, this is software that permits individuals to send private, unsolicited messages to other online users, and receive responses on the private channel which has been established.

3.1.12 Private rooms

A subset of a chat room, which may or may not have a restricted number of participants. The users of a private room may also have some control over who can enter the room.

4 Relating Stories and Examples

In the discussion, you will be giving examples to your child. Relate them in a simple and straightforward manner. The first example is to illustrate the dangers of meeting strangers on the Internet. The second example illustrates the dangers of viewing or downloading sites or files with graphic images of violence, sex, or promoting drug use. You can use these sample discussions, or change the particulars if you have a story to tell from your own experience. After telling the story, you will ask questions and offer guidance to your children if they do not know the correct answers. But you may be surprised how easily they understand the problem in the story, and can instinctively discover many of the right steps to take.

I have included the answers in italics for you, the parent, to use in the discussion.

▶ 4.1 The First Sample Story

Meredith is a young girl who has gone online and is visiting a chat room. She meets a boy, "David." They begin to chat with each other. They discover that they both enjoy kites and belong to the same kite club. "David" explains that he has an amazing new kite, and asks for her address so that he can stop by to show it to her. "David" sends along his address and a picture, to encourage her to share. [Note: You can vary the scenario as you wish, and may include situations such as "David" asking for a picture, or to meet.]

4.1.1 Questions

1. **What should Meredith do?**

   Relate that she is not allowed to send out her picture to anyone without first getting permission from her parents. Let the other person know that she will ask her parents and let "David" know if she can send her picture.

2. **What is going on, and how does Meredith feel?**
   Is she convinced that "David" is her friend and the person in the picture that she received?

3. **Could "David" really be a forty-year-old man?**
   In many cases, yes, "David" did turn out to be an older man.

4. **Why would "David" lie?**
   To trick Meredith into giving away personal information.

5. **Who might be pictured in the photo "David" sent? Could it be a picture of a little boy "David" has hurt in the past?**
   Or just some picture he found on the Internet and is now using to hide behind.

6. **What can "David" do with Meredith's address?**
   Did you know he could find Meredith's home, and then sit outside her home waiting for her to come out?

7. **If "David" asks for a picture, what should Meredith do?**
   Let "David" know that she is asking her parents about sending a picture.

8. **What if "David" asks to meet Meredith?**
   Meredith should tell him no, that she is letting her parents know he asked to meet and if they say it is okay, then maybe they could meet.

9. **Who should Meredith talk with about "David"?**

   Her parents.

10. **If someone like David contacts you, what are the rules of the family concerning strangers?**

    *We do not talk with them, we do not go with them, and we tell Mom and Dad if a stranger asks a personal question, or asks us to go with them. **Know these rules, and post them by the computer.***

▶ 4.2 The Second Sample Story

Jack is a young boy who has gone online late one night and past his bedtime. He meets a new friend, "Peter," online. "Peter" suggests he visit a fun, new Web site. "Peter" sends a link. When Jack clicks on the link, he finds pictures of smiling, naked boys.

4.2.1 Questions

1. **What should Jack do?**

   Log off immediately and tell his parents how Peter tricked him. Make sure your children know that even though they were up late, in violation of the rules, they can still talk to you about what happened. Make sure they understand that they were wrong to be up late, but since they told you about it you are moderating what punishment they would have gotten had they not told you. Remember, do not overreact and ruin the trust you are developing with your children.

2. **What is going on, and how does Jack feel?**

   Talk with your children about what just happened and how they would feel if they saw such things.

3. **Who might his new friend be?**

   He could be Mr. Stranger Danger.

4. **Why would "Peter" lie?**

   Could he be trying to trick Jack and cause Jack to get in trouble or could he even want to do the things seen in the pictures to Jack?

5. **If "Peter" contacts him again, what should Jack do?**

   Jack should tell him that what he did was wrong, and that Jack told his parents. That Jack and his parents decided not to talk with Peter anymore online. Then put Peter on "ignore" (or whatever the term your service uses) so that he cannot see Jack online anymore.

6. **What if "Peter" asks to meet Jack?**

   Jack should say no, and tell his parents.

7. **Who should he talk with about "Peter"?**

   His parents, and right away.

8. **If Jack talks to his friend, Miguel, first, and Miguel says he shouldn't tell his parents because they might get mad, what should Jack do?**

   Tell Miguel that he knows his parents will listen and not get mad. They will discuss the problem with Jack and work out a solution. Tell Miguel that lying to his parents or keeping secrets from his parents would get Jack in more trouble than talking to "Peter" would have.

9. **If someone like "Peter" contacts you, what are the rules of the family concerning strangers?**

    We do not talk with them, we do not go with them, and we tell Mom and Dad if a stranger asks a personal question, or asks us to go with them. **Know these rules, and post them by the computer.**

5 The Review

Great job! The discussion is over. Whew! After you have related your stories and discussed them with your child, reinforce four key points for them.

a. The Internet is a wonderful place for education and entertainment, but there are family rules that must be followed. You are getting older and want to do more things; the way you earn those things is by showing how responsible and trustworthy you can be.

b. Always talk to us, or your teacher while at school, if anything happens to you while online that makes you feel uncomfortable. Never be afraid that we will be mad at you for what happened, everyone makes mistakes. It's how you deal with the mistakes that show whether you are grown up and responsible or not.

c. Never ever give out your last name, address, picture, or telephone number to anyone online unless they are personally known to you and your parents have given you permission to give the information to that person.

d. Never ever give out any family information such as credit card numbers, address, pictures, last name, or the names of your brothers or sisters online.

6 Making an Online Contract

This is one of the most useful tools I know of to help you instill in your child's mind and heart a good sense of rights and responsibilities when it comes to the Internet. This can be used to help reinforce the rules you have agreed on and can be posted on the side of the monitor. One such online contract can be found at

http://www.ag.state.il.us/programs/
familyinternetsafety/fismain.htm.

This is courtesy of Jim Ryan, the Illinois Attorney General, and is free for downloading. The site contains one contract for home and one contract for students and teachers that can be used at school. You can reproduce the contract in any number needed for home, classroom, town hall meeting, or homeowners meetings.

AGREEMENT
TO ABIDE BY THE RULES

PARENTS: PLEASE DISCUSS THIS AGREEMENT WITH YOUR CHILDREN, SIGN IT TOGETHER AND POST IT NEAR YOUR COMPUTER.

I WILL not give out personal information such as my address, telephone number, parents' work addresses/telephone numbers, or the name of my school without my parents' permission.

I WILL tell my parents right away if I come across information that makes me feel uncomfortable.

I WILL never agree to get together with someone I "meet" online without first checking with my parents. If my parents agree to the meeting, I will be sure that it is in a public place and bring my mother or father along.

I WILL never send a person my picture or anything else without first checking with my parents.

I WILL not respond to any messages that are mean or in any way make me feel uncomfortable. It is not my fault if I get a message like that. If I do, I will tell my parents right away so they can contact the online service.

I WILL talk with my parents so that we can set up rules for going online. We will decide upon the time of day that I can be online, the length of time I can be online, and appropriate areas for me to visit. I will not access other areas or break these rules without their permission.

_____   _____
CHILD   **PARENT(S)**

Illinois Attorney General Jim Ryan • Illinois PTA
Report Internet child exploitation to www.ag.state.il.us

These rules are excerpted and reprinted from *Child Safety on the Information Superhighway* by Lawrence J. Magid. They are reprinted with permission of the National Center for Missing and Exploited Children (NCMEC). Copyright © NCMEC 1994. All rights reserved.

For those of you who can't read small print (like me!), here is what the agreement says.

Agreement to Abide by the Rules

Parents, please discuss this Agreement with your children. Sign it together and post it near the computer.

I WILL not give out personal information such as my address, telephone number, parent's work address or telephone number, or the name of my school without my parents' permission.

I WILL tell my parents right away if I come across information that makes me feel uncomfortable.

I WILL never agree to get together with someone I "meet" online without first checking with my parents. If my parents agree to the meeting, I will be sure that it is a public place and bring my mother and father along.

I WILL never send a person my picture or anything else without first checking with my parents.

I WILL not respond to any messages that are mean or in any way make me feel uncomfortable. It is not by fault if I get a message like that. If I do, I will tell my parents right away so they can contact the online service.

I WILL talk with my parents so that we can set up rules for going online. We will decide upon the time of day that I can be online, the length of time I can be online, and appropriate areas for me to visit. I will not access other areas or break these rules without their permission.

7 After the Discussion

▶ 7.1 Review your current online safety controls

The first thing you may want to do after your online chat is to review the controls you have available to you through your hardware, software, or Internet service provider. We'll cover this in the next few chapters. This is where having your child show you where he or she visited and how he or she uses the Internet can give you some peace of mind. If they accidentally go to the wrong area and your software filters the content from being seen you will feel good. If you have not configured the software properly, you will learn with your child sitting right next to you and you can correct your mistakes.

You may also wish to install protective software. You may find that the controls from your service provider do not match up to the options provided by other programs on the market. This way, if your children access an inappropriate area, the software will protect them and you can discuss why the software was activated.

Your child will realize that the software activation is not a bad thing, but a protection for them.

▶ 7.2 Watch for warning signs concerning your child's online activity

1. Is your child online late at night?

2. Is the online activity excessive (over two hours on average per day)? This, of course, is not school- or homework-related online time. As a parent, I realize that we are losing more and more of our children's at home time to homework.

3. Is your child alone for most of the time during his or her online sessions?

4. Is your child spending the majority of his or her time online in chat rooms?

5. Is your child reluctant to talk about or evasive in describing his or her online experiences?

6. Does your child minimize the screen on the computer when you walk by? Or do you notice several programs showing in the task bar at the bottom of the screen, but no programs active on the monitor? This is a sure sign that something your child does not want you to see is hiding in the task bar.

8 Taking Action

If you see one or more warning signs, take action immediately. Have a follow-up discussion with your child, reinforcing that nothing she tells you will make her look bad in your eyes. Make sure you use every effort to open up communication with her about online experiences, and keep those lines open.

However, do not forget you are the parent and sometimes that means the unpopular job is yours. That means you may have to restrict or take away your child's online time if he or she refuses to obey the rules. It is a tough job, but you're the parent and it's the right thing to do to protect your child.

You may also consider a more careful supervision of his or her online activity. Review the chapter on supervising for a full outline of how to approach this.

If you see any hint of contact with an online predator, be sure to talk with your child immediately and get in contact with local law enforcement. You will not only be protecting your child, but also other children the predator will exploit in the future.

3

Child Protection Software

OVERVIEW

What You Will Learn

- The various flavors of safety software on the market, from controls supplied with your Internet browser, to software programs downloadable from the Internet.

How You Will Feel

- In control of your browser, and aware of your options to increase your peace of mind by buying and installing additional protection software.

What Is Covered

- Parental controls offered by Internet service providers
- Blocking style protection software
- Content Filtering protection software
- Cyber Sentinel
- Special notes for AOL subscribers
- The problem of private chat rooms
- Instant messages
- Instant Messenger
- Power Tools and Power Plus for AOL Instant Messenger
- How software helps law enforcement catch online redators
- McAfee Visual Trace
- Why our best defense is education

Detective Mike's Third Law

If you want to play major-league ball,
you need a major-league mitt.
Use strong protection at all times.

---

1 Parental Controls Supplied By the Internet Service Provider

Parental controls are supplied through the Internet service, and there is a range of controls available. Family-oriented services such as AOL offer a more extensive set of controls, while smaller or niche ISPs may offer only a rudimentary set of controls.

▶ 1.1 The on/off control

Most controls are of the *on or off* variety. You have the option to switch on, or switch off, various features of the Internet service. Examples include:

1. Do you want your child to have e-mail?
2. Do you want your child to access the Internet?

1.1.1 Why on/off controls do not work

The problem with on/off controls is that children will find away around them. Experienced parents know that children test them all the time. The Internet is a perfect opportunity for your child to re-stage that eternal battle for control, and test their limits. Why? The Internet is, essentially, a solo medium as opposed to an all-family activity.

Telling a child *"You cannot do that"* is like throwing down the gauntlet. You might as well say, *"I dare you to defy me and find a way to do that."* They will find away around the *off* part.

To put it accurately, children find ways around *most* of the software. Not all of it. I have seen this tactic fail time after time with children at home, in the library, or at school.

I believe there are four reasons for this.

1. Our children are determined and creative.

2. On/off controls can give the parent, teacher, or librarian a false sense of security. I have had countless discussions with professional educators on this subject, and when I have asked them about situations that can

come up with children and the Internet, a typical answer is, "Children can't do that here."

3. Because the controls are so easy to manage, the task of managing them is often handed off to underpaid, overworked, under-experienced educators.

   The fact that I remember black and white television, record players and clamp-on old-fashioned roller skates with four wheels not in line, doesn't mean that I don't trust people under thirty. However, there are many young educators, who have no children themselves, who are placed in charge of Internet safety. Many of them are barely out of their teens themselves and have not become accustomed to being on the authority side of the age-old struggle between adults and children. This leads them to underestimate the determination and creativity of our children, which leads us right back to reason #1.

4. The fact is that I have come to believe that many professionals are threatened by the presence of the police in their workplace, especially when law enforcement is giving advice on the management of technology. In fact, most people feel intimidated when a police officer shows up and begins to discuss a problem at their work place. All of which leads people to avoid contacting the police for help in designing online safety procedures. This can lead to situations where children are left relatively unprotected.

The good news is that, once you establish an understanding, these can be some of the most helpful and instructive people you will ever interact with. One school district's information service is a perfect example.

The first time I was called to the district they were apprehensive about what I would do with their system, how it would impact the school district, and their liability.

For my part, I was a little intimidated because I knew these people all knew infinitely more about technology than I did; in fact, all of them had earned degrees in management of information systems.

As we all sat down and began discussing what occurred, where the evidence of the activity was located, how to recover the evidence, and ultimately how the case would be investigated most of the concerns were taken care of on both sides. We began to trust each other and understand that the police were not going to come into their work place and mangle or destroy their system. During this time, we developed a new method of investigating cases involving technology.

As we discovered additional information about the event and the offender, we continually re-assessed the merits of the case, keeping in mind our ultimate goal of protecting the children in the district.

Was this a student with a clean record, or a real troublemaker? Just how serious of a break of the rules or systems had occurred? Would there be damage to the victim in making the event publicly know? Would there be further damage to the victim? Was this break of the rules worth a formal prosecution, or adjudication through less formal systems, or even discipline at the school level?

Today they are my favorite system to deal with and the

method of re-evaluating the ultimate outcome of a case has become the normal procedure for our department.

That is the highlight, but there is a less cooperative side.

I have had a number of discussions with Internet service providers that go badly. I ask them, "Do you have controls in place helping parents to protect their children?"

The reply is often, "We have a control that parents can set, allowing their children to have access to the Internet, or not."

I ask, "Why would a parent pay you for Internet access for their child so they can get the necessary research for homework assignments and then say 'no' to having their child access the Internet?"

It's not an idle question. According to leading researchers, adults who have children under sixteen are twice as likely to have Internet access at home than parents without younger children.

The answer from the ISP is typically, "They can access the Internet when their parents are sitting next to them, by going through their parents account."

This is my point about experience with children. Not too many parents have the extra time after work, before dinner, or even after dinner to get online together and research the Internet. Once in awhile? Sure. But every night? No way.

Besides, that leaves children starting their homework at, say, 8 o'clock in the evening. Perhaps not finishing until 10 or 11!

The reason we got the Internet was to make life easier, not to delay the start of homework until Mom and Dad are available. We want our kids to do their homework before dinner so we can spend our precious family time together on activities we all enjoy.

▶ 1.2 Using browser settings to control access to nudity, language, and violence

The typical ISP, in addition to offering on/off controls, will offer a browser that controls access to inappropriate sites. Many corporations, in fact, use this feature to control the amount of access their employees have to inappropriate or time-wasting content.

Their software works with the browser and will not allow children to enter sites that have ratings that you, the parent, have set as unacceptable. These ratings and settings can be found in the *Internet Options* section of your browser.

In your browser options you can set the level of appropriateness by selecting the type of language, sex, violence, and nudity. The browser will read the type of site that your child is attempting to view and block those that fall in the categories you want to block.

Sounds pretty foolproof, right?

1.2.1 Why browser settings do not work

What is the first thing that enterprising kids say when they see that a handful of browser settings stand between them and the Web sites they are curious to explore?

Kewl.

That's "cool" to me and you. Here's what they can, and will, do.

1. They connect to the ISP, link to the Internet, and access a perfectly safe and legitimate Web site. For example, *www.disney.go.com*. From the ISP's point of view (and in the browser's session record), they are logged for a safe and family-oriented session with Mickey, Donald, Minnie, and the gang.

2. Meanwhile, they use the Internet connection to launch a chat program like IRC Chat. Every ISP in the world can support two simultaneous Internet sessions. Typically these are both handled through the browser. But smart kids can be mighty sneaky. And a surprising number of them figure this out.

Children didn't change with the arrival of the Internet. They will always test boundaries, and won't always show the best judgment. It doesn't matter whether the boundary is based on dress, attitude, activities, friends, or the Internet. It is part of being a child, growing and learning.

The difference here is that it's relatively easy to spot a kid with a spiked Mohawk, or a newfound interest in controversial music. It's impossible to spot a kid running a chat session and a "Fun with Mickey" session at the same time on the Internet. The statistics show Mickey only, but experience tells us otherwise.

I worked on a case with a group of junior high school students who were using the school computer lab to run afoul of school policies and, unfortunately, several laws.

When we spoke with the staff at the school district we were told "Not possible; you can't do that on our system."

By this time I had interviewed the students involved, so I asked for permission to demonstrate what they had shown me.

Seven taps of the keyboard later, we all saw the hole in the system. The controls on the school system were of the on/off type, and easy to get around. The presence of the controls had lulled the school officials into a false sense of security and into lax supervision. The kids had the time and the motivation to get around the controls, and off they went into dangerous ground.

▶ 1.3 The bottom line

We didn't have our kids just for the tax breaks. We had them to enjoy them, and we intend to protect them. On/off controls simply leave us with a set of bad choices, overly taxing supervision schedules, and sometimes a false sense of security that not only kids, but predators, take advantage of.

2 Other Controls Supplied By Outside Companies

▶ 2.1 Blocking software

There are two types of *blocking* software on the market, but they work in essentially the same way. The developer of the software adds the names of sites to a list that is managed by the software.

The first type of blocking software is the *black list*. The software developer is adding the names and addresses of offensive sites, and the software blocks access to those offensive sites by a computer whenever the software is installed.

The second type involves *white lists*. Instead of adding the names of forbidden sites, it adds the names of acceptable sites. In this type of blocking, your child can only surf out to sites that have been deemed appropriate by the software manufacturer.

2.1.1 The weaknesses of blocking software

Although superior in concept to on/off controls, here are three critical weaknesses that make blocking software unsatisfactory.

1. The Internet is a dynamic environment and Web sites and their addresses change by the minute. This type of software requires the parent to update daily by going to a list at the software's home page and getting the new lists of white and black lists. Update every day? Just what we need. Mars has a twenty-five-hour day, and sometimes I think the developers must live there, where everyone has an extra hour for this chore.

2. This type of blocking software works off of your browser, and it is subject to the same problem as on/off controls are when kids learn to access a legitimate "allowed" site with the browser and then access

an illicit site by running a different program, such as chat software.

3. There is another technique that was designed specifically to get around this type of blocking software. Have you ever clicked on a page when all of a sudden several other pages open up? Sometimes they are ads. Frequently they are completely different Web sites. Sometimes your computer goes crazy and launches page after page—very often with content you didn't want to know existed. Then when you try to hit the back button you can't get back to your original page.

This is called *portaling*. When you accessed the site (perhaps innocently off an e-mail announcement), the site closed off the link to your browser and at the same time, probably the link to your blocking software. Then it gave you a new browser to shop with, their browser, which had a very different idea of what was appropriate to see on your computer.

4. Most blocking software does not deal with word processing or e-mail text. Don't we also want to block graphic e-mail, death threats, and harassing text in word-processing documents? If you are using blocking software you are probably going to have to purchase additional software to monitor e-mail, word processing, and harassment. Most children are smart enough to know that the school system will monitor Web traffic and where the browser is visiting.

5. Blocking software does not prevent the download of sophisticated viruses. Your school system will in all

likelihood have software that prevents the download-ing of .exe files. These are the usual virus carriers. But how many of us are smart enough to spot Trojan horses that arrive with innocent looking names and extensions?

6. Children are becoming more and more clever. In one case I was involved with, several virus and highly ob-jectionable files were brought into the school's system from the Internet, several with the .exe extension.

When I talked to the children involved, they ex-plained that when they first tried to bring the files into the system, they were blocked because the system saw the extension .exe and related that it was an unac-ceptable download.

After several tries, the children learned that if they renamed the file they wanted to bring down to an ac-ceptably-named file, then the software would not block the download and allow the file to come onto the school's system. For example, the file notepad.exe is a file found on the windows system. So when the children renamed a video game about a student that uses an AK-47 submachine gun to kill the teacher and students in the class the schools software did not block it.

7. Typically, blocking software has poor reporting and notification reports. It is difficult to find blocking software that provides parents a timely and concise notification of violations each day, letting parents know they should check the log for the blocking soft-

ware. Or, there is a notification, but every violation is listed and the parent is forced to weed out the ones that mean trouble and are not just accidental clicks on hidden links.

▶ 2.2 Content filtering software

This is the software of choice. It allows parents to choose the content that is acceptable to view on their computer. A good version of this software works on the browser, the word processor, Web pages, and e-mail. It reads everything your computer does and helps edit what your child sees.

This software can be tailored to specifically help your family. You add your last name, your telephone number, your credit card numbers, the name of the school your child attends, and other personal information you do not want transmitted to the Internet by your child. The software reads what is being said and blocks the personal information from being sent out.

Content filtering is not foolproof. Our smart friend at the ISP might tell us: "Any kid who is smart enough to get around blocking software is smart enough to get around content filtering. They use code words so no one will know what he or she is saying."

No question about it. I have seen children using code words, words like the emoticons we talked about earlier, or codes like:

POS parent over shoulder

TA teacher alert

PA parent alert

CTN can't talk now

911 emergency stop

And these codes make filtering software less effective. Based on real life experiences with my children, the children on sports teams I have coached, and from interaction with hundreds of children at schools being taught Internet safety, I believe that children are not disciplined in their Internet behavior—eventually they make mistakes and the software will catch that mistake.

The key difference between content filtering and blocking software is that with blocking software you need to be clever just once to figure out a way around the program— with content filtering the child has to be clever all the time.

Also, predators do not know the software is on your child's machine at the onset of a conversation. In the twelve years I have been involved in computer investigations I have not once seen a predator ask a child: "Do you have any software on your machine that will tell your parents what we are chatting about?"

In fact, even if a predator were as smart as that, it wouldn't help him much. The type of software we will look at can be programmed to catch that phrase. In essence, this makes the act of trying not to get caught the actual thing that catches the predator.

In short, our experience is that content filtering works if the predator *or* the child fails to diligently work around it all the time, and we have learned that in real life those mistakes do happen.

The trick is to pick the software that will best protect your child. I have tried several, and the one I would recommend is Cyber Sentinel. This product includes both types of protective actions, site blocking and filtering technologies. The product also allows the parent to select just what times the Internet can be accessed. Let's take a look at what this software can accomplish.

▶ 2.3 Cyber Sentinel

First, let's look at the filtering part of the software, which I believe is the most important feature of Cyber Sentinel. The best feature of Cyber Sentinel is that it is parent friendly.

Anyone can load the software, select the password, and set the configuration. As I go through the different steps, I will include screen captures (geek speak for pictures) of how to do each step. This will help in loading the software and selecting the proper configuration for your family.

First you want to click on the setup file for Cyber Sentinel. The software will install and load the different libraries.

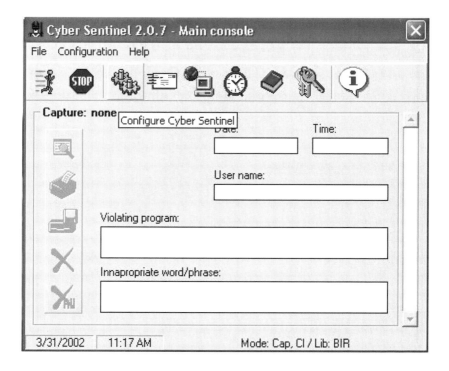

After the software has loaded, you can select how you would like it to run.

First, decide if you want it in the *active* or *stealth* mode. In the *active* mode, the software will allow for different types of captures and warning screens.

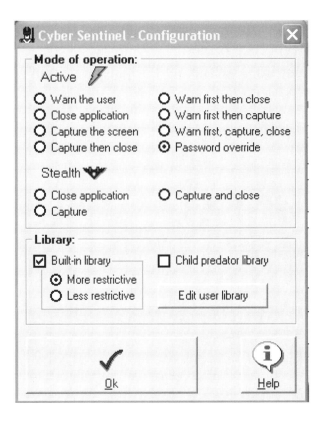

If you select the active mode and run the software with the password override, your child will know the software is present on the machine. I personally recommend this setting. Tell your child about the software and why it's on your machine. Be straight forward in telling your child that sometimes bad people on the Internet will try to make your child's browser go to areas of the Internet that are inappropriate. The software is there to help prevent this and if something happens and he or she is sent to an inappropriate place, the software will step in and block that material from being viewed.

The software actually goes out to the site before showing

it on your monitor. It pre-reads the page to see if the content is appropriate or not. If the material is inappropriate then the software steps in and displays a warning sign that the material is prohibited.

The software informs the child that the page has information on it that is not allowed and has caused a violation. The child needs to have Mom or Dad enter the password to clear the warning screen.

In the background, unseen by your child, the software takes a screen capture (picture) of the offending page and stores it in a hidden file that Mom and Dad can review at a later time.

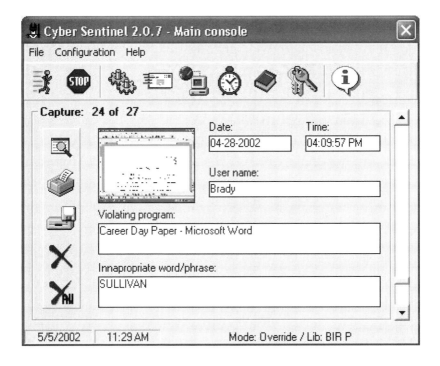

The screen shows the parent the date of the violation, the time of the violation, the user on the computer who caused the violation, and what program was being used. In this example it is Microsoft Word and the violation is *Sullivan*.

The nice thing about this type of software is that it does not log everything your child does online, and then make you edit the log looking for violations. It only logs the violations that occur due to the parameters you set on your own machine.

No outside agency, government, or software company tells you what your child should or should not see. Parents make those decisions. As Mom or Dad, you can access the violations and see exactly what caused the program to trip and do a screen capture. The software displays the actual wording that caused the problem. It gives you a picture of the offending page or Web site and the date and time the violation occurred.

The software will also send you an e-mail if you want, and notify you of the violation on your home machine in a real-time method. The e-mail only tells you that there was a violation and does not send the violation along. This is to be sure you do not have a problem if the violation includes pornographic material—pretty difficult material to explain on your work computer!

As the parent, you can review the violations and know which ones you need to discuss with your child. Not all violations need a discussion.

I use this product on my own machine at home, and my wife and I have a sense of safety for our children on the Internet. We did as recommended and put in our last name, address, telephone number, and things I will demonstrate later. However, this program is one that reads all actions on your computer—your browser, your ISP, e-mail, and word processing program. This product is an all-inclusive aid to protecting your child.

In our first encounter, our son launched Microsoft Word to use as a word processing program to write a school paper. We forgot that one of the first things he needs to enter on his paper is his whole name. When he typed his last name the software stepped in and he saw the warning screen. We did not want his full name going out to the Internet, but we never thought about having to use his name for homework.

So when we use Cyber Sentinel, our son does his assignment first, then asks either his mother or I to turn off the software. He then types his full name, prints the document, saves the file, and we turn the software back on.

We don't mind the extra step because it's so important to have software that protects children from inappropriate content that comes in via word processing files.

As I discussed earlier in the chapter, without protection software that works at this level, it is too easy for the curious and inventive child to get around the software, and for predators too.

One of the easiest ways to accomplish this is to open a word processing program, type in the harassing language you want to send—or the death threat or a link to a forbidden site—then attach the word processing text to the e-mail as an attachment. The software on the browser never sees inside the attachment so it does not know the nature of the attachment.

For example, your child receives an e-mail message that reads:

HOMEWORK HELP HOTLINE. *Here is a link to a Web site that will help you with your algebra homework.*

Inside the message is a link to an inappropriate site. Your child does not realize that this is a link to a harmful site, and clicks on the link. The site itself is harmless-looking, but it launches a second browser window filled with inappropriate content.

This technique fools browser protection software, but not content filtering such as Cyber Sentinel. The content filter follows the link, reads the site and its content, and depending on the speed of your computer's processor and the speed of the Internet connection, the page starts to load or may not load at all, and the warning page is seen. It blocks the page from being viewed by your child, but you are able to see the violation in the screen capture when you use your password to review the violations.

In this case, your child is going to explain what happened and that he or she did not know it was a bad site. Redirecting children to areas they never meant to visit is a common practice in e-mail, in chat sessions, and on Web sites.

3 Setting up Cyber Sentinel or Other Content Filtering Software

When setting up the software, it will help you in picking what type of content you want to filter. Cyber Sentinel has three different libraries you can use. You can use one, all three, or any combination of the three.

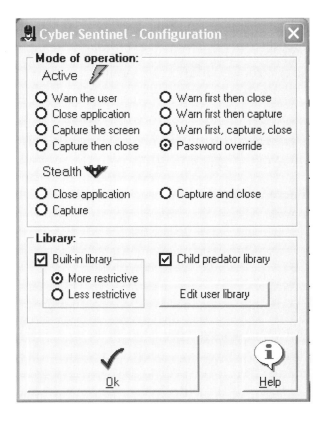

The first library was constructed around violence and sexually explicit language. This will prevent your child from seeing sexually explicit Web sites, e-mail messages, or chat rooms and instant message/private messages. The software takes the place of Mom and Dad and stops children from using language that they know their mothers would not approve of. But also it keeps them out of explicit sites, or protects them when predators use explicit language with them.

The second library was designed to look for common phrases used by predators to lure children away from their homes. This library, constructed with the help of law enforcement, is geared toward keeping your child safe from those predators online looking to victimize children. The software looks for the type of language that predators would use to groom children for victimization.

These are a series of questions used by predators that allow the predators to establish the likelihood of getting caught chatting to this child. These questions, discussed in detail in Part One, "The Online Predator," include:

1. "Where is your computer located?

   Who would really care about where your child's computer is located? Someone who is about to say something inappropriate and send graphic images that are highly objectionable. He wants to know if the computer is in the family room or kitchen where he knows Mom or Dad or a brother or sister will see the material.

2. Who uses your computer?

   The predator is trying to gauge his vulnerability to being caught by finding out just how many people use the computer and may see whatever the predator send.

These questions can give the predator an idea of how vulnerable your child may be and help him decide if he should start grooming this child. Make no mistake, I am a police officer, not a psychiatrist or therapist for sexual offenders, but I have seen these techniques used over and over again. They are all too often successful in allowing the predator to gain access to a child

The third library is a blank one in which you should enter information to customize the software for your family. In this library, you can enter your last name, address, telephone number, the name of the school your child attends, and your credit card numbers.

If you wish to go online and purchase items at Web sites, you can use a password to override the software to allow the release of your credit card information.

In this example, the default password *cyber* is used to turn off the software. Do not forget to change the default password once you have the software installed. It is simple to do. Click on *Password* and you will get the password box.

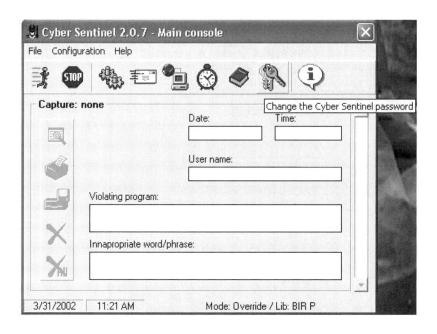

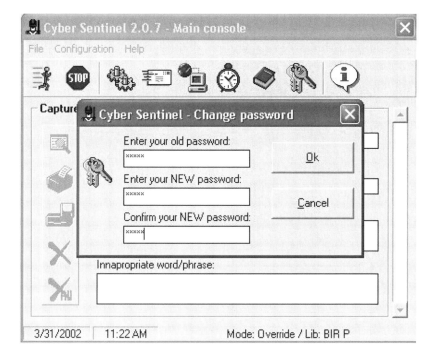

Enter your old password and then select a new password. Enter the password twice to confirm the change and click OK. The password is now changed.

By entering personal information, if your child forgets the family rules about private information, or a predator tricks them—and the predators can be very good at persuading the children to do things—the software is sitting there to protect them.

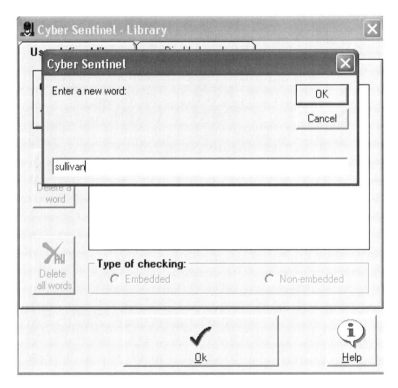

Each word is added separately, and then is saved to the database of the software. You can choose as much or as little information as you are comfortable with. Remember, the recommendation is for your last name, telephone number, name of your child's school, and home address.

The software does not care how persuasive the predator is.

Also, we have seen from experience that even if children are using codes in the chat room while having inappropriate conversations, eventually someone will trip the software by forgetting to use a coded phrase. People are just not consistent enough, especially children.

One of my favorite features of Cyber Sentinel is the fact that it reads chat and private messages on IRC (Internet Relay Chat) and MSN Messenger and America Online Instant Message and Instant Messenger.

For those of you who were thinking, "Well my child is pretty computer literate. What if they turn off the software?" Well, if junior tries to turn off the software it will send you a message telling you that junior tried to turn off the software. This is a big mistake, and usually results in being grounded from the computer for a period of time. Honest mistakes are one thing and should be discussed—you need not overreact. But a deliberate attempt to get around the software is a major no-no in our household.

4 Cyber Sentinel in the Stealth Mode

Everything we have discussed above occurs in the *active* mode. In the *stealth* mode, the software does the same filtering—the screen captures are being logged and the e-mail notifications are being sent out—but there is no warning screen seen and no icon in the status box showing the software is working.

My son has gotten to the point that when a mistake does occur, my office phone usually rings before the e-mail can even get to me. He knows that as long as it was a mistake and he let's us know it's not a big deal. In fact, most of the mistakes center on private information being used. He forgets when chatting with a friend and mentions his school or school team by name, or one of his friends uses one of those bad words. And I have to admit the phone call from my son helps lighten my day at the police department most of the time.

5 Other Cyber Sentinel Features

▶ 5.1 Blocking

The software also has the ability to block Internet sites if you care to use that feature. You can bring up the configuration panel and add the sites you want blocked.

Blocking doesn't work very well, in my experience, but the feature is there if you want it.

▶ 5.2 Time Management

The software will allow you to pick what time of the day and for how long the Internet can be accessed. In the *configuration panel*, select *time management*, and then select the times you will allow your child to access the Internet.

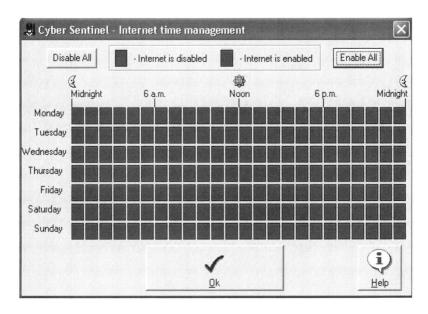

The rule here is no different then what I used to hear from my own father many, many years ago. When I would go out with a friend, I had a curfew. He would tell me to be home by 10, and of course, I would ask for 11 and we would argue (a very short argument!) and he would reply that "there is nothing you can do after 10 that you can't do before 10, except get in trouble." I was home by 10.

This is a good rule with the Internet.

Later in the night, there is less and less child-oriented material in chat rooms and private messages. The child-safe

Web sites (look in the resource section of this book for several of these sites) don't change their content, but other areas do change as the night gets later. Setting the controls for prime homework time, some fun time after homework, and some time on the weekends is a good guide.

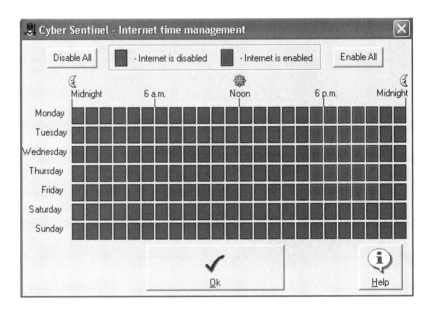

In this configuration, the Inherent is available from dinnertime till ten at night. The addition of some weekend time would also be acceptable. You simply click on the time frame you want open and it turns from red to green. If you are having trouble with your child you can prohibit access to the Internet at any time by configuring the time management.

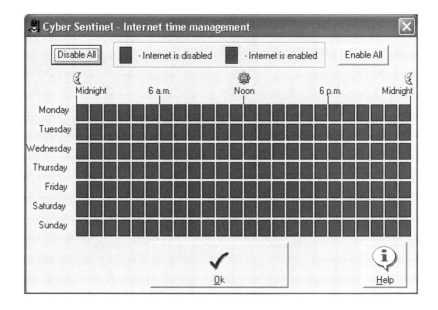

That much *red* has to have an effect on your child. You can find a trial version of Cyber Sentinel at *www. cybersentinel.com*.

6 Especially for America Online Subscribers

Congratulations! You are subscribing to one of the best-moderated chat communities on the Internet. Contrary to what people hear or think, America Online does spend a large amount of time and effort to keep the chat rooms safe and clean. There are both moderated and un-moderated chat rooms. Nonetheless, the rooms are relatively safe.

Even if there is not a *community leader* moderating the chat, AOL has *bots* on all its chat sites. A bot is like a little cyber space robot or script written to prevent anyone from creating a chat room with a name that would signify illegal content.

For example, I've discussed the different chat rooms you could access on IRC (Internet Relay Chat). There were several "Preteen" chat rooms where the trading of images of children, under the age of thirteen years old engaging in sexual activities was taking place.

However, if you tried to create a chat room on America Online called "Pre" or "Preteen," you would receive a warning from America Online stating that the type of conduct that occurs in rooms of that name is a violation of America Online terms of service. If this was your second attempt at creating such an area on America Online, your account would be terminated.

America Online tries hard to keep their system a clean and healthy environment, while balancing this with not being overbearing or taking on a censorship role.

7 The Problem with Private Chat Rooms

A private chat room is somewhat like an instant message. It creates a private space for "conversation" where both sides of the chat are displayed. However, the private chat room can be enjoyed by more than two people at a time. In fact up to twenty-three people can be in an AOL private chat room.

Every private chat room is given a name by its creator. To enter the room, you have to know the name. Although the public chat rooms on AOL are always listed in a live public directory showing the title of the room and how many people are currently chatting there, private rooms are not listed.

But it is possible to accidentally stumble into a private room.

Here's how you do it. Look on your AOL console for this icon and click on it.

The following box will appear.

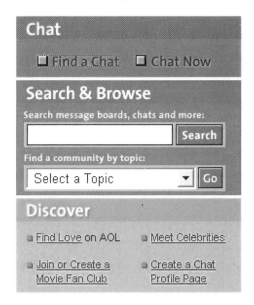

Click on *Find a Chat* and it will take you to:

Click on *Enter a Private Chat*. Here's what you see.

At this box you would type in the name of the private chat room you want to enter. This is where you have to know exactly what the name of the room is in order to join. The person who created the room would normally supply this.

If I was just to enter a series of names, I might stumble upon the name of a room that was created, joining the room if it were not already full. In this manner, someone other than those invited into the room can view the private chat.

Now remember, if I try to create an obviously illegal room, the bot will catch it and prevent it from happening on America Online. Your children are being protected from creating such rooms or seeing undesirable content, such as the sort of IRC chat rooms I've discussed, by the basic features of America Online.

8 Instant Messages

AOL subscribers are usually familiar with *instant messaging*. It is a form of e-mail or private conversation. Two AOL subscribers can exchange messages instantaneously in a special pop-up window which keeps a record of the entire conversation during the time it is active. The conversation is private. The instant message feature is hugely popular and is now available via many other ISPs. Once the instant message is closed, the data is not retrievable without the use of forensic software.

9 The Difference between an Instant Message and Instant Messenger

In an instant message conversation, both individuals are America Online subscribers. This means your children have AOL and so do their friends. In fact, they can put their friends' screen names into a *Buddy List* that will notify them whenever these friends come online. If a friend is online, his name will appear on the buddy list and your children can send him an instant message (IM) to say hello or chat.

But if they have a friend who uses another service provider, that friend probably uses the program Instant Messenger. This allows people from outside America On-line to add their friends from America Online to their buddy lists. When their friends are online they can see their names on the buddy list and send them a request to start an instant messenger session.

The look of the request is different. Within AOL, when

you want to send an IM you just open up the box and fire away. On the other person's screen, the box just opens up and you see the chat.

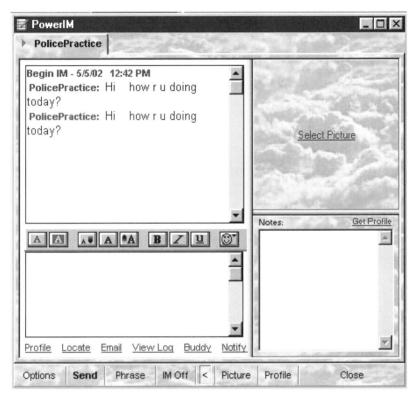

With Instant Messenger, the person on AOL will see a box asking if he or she wishes to accept the request for an instant messenger session, and gives the screen name of the person asking for the session. The AOL member can accept the request and chat, or ignore.

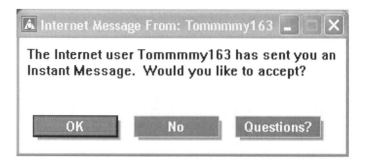

AOL is not the only ISP to have this type of service. On MSN it is called Windows Messenger, however, Power Plus is only compatible with America Online's Instant Messenger.

1 0 Power Tools or Power Plus for AOL Instant Messenger

This product. made by BPS Software, costs about $30 and is invaluable for parents who want to know with whom their children are chatting and what is said.

With Power Tools for America Online or Power Plus for AIM installed on your computer, you can use your word processor to read any chat conversation your child has had. The program opens a file on the hard drive every time a chat room or instant message or messenger session is started.

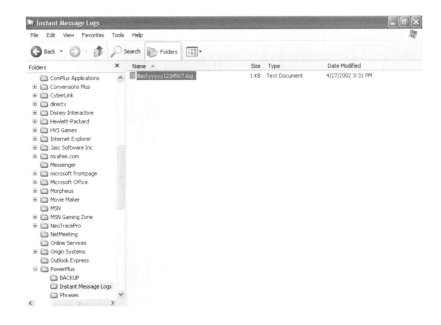

It dates and times the beginning of the conversation, records the conversation in its entirety, and then dates and times the closing of the session. By navigating with your word processor to the proper file, you can view the conversation.

▶ 10.1 Using Power Tools

In the case of Power Tools for America Online, launch your word processor and direct it to open a file. Navigate to your hard drive (usually C:) and then navigate down the root of the C drive to program files. Expand the Program Files directory, navigate down to Power Tools, and expand the Power Tools directory. You will see subfolders for chat rooms and instant message logs. By expanding these directories you will see the names of the rooms your child visited and what was said. You can also navigate to the Instant Message Logs folder and see the entire text of an instant message conversation between your child and someone from America Online.

▶ 10.2 Using Power Plus for AOL Instant Messenger

To use Power Plus, go to the C: drive, then to Program Files, then to Power Plus, and then to Instant Message Logs.

This program does not have a notification feature and it does not have security built in to prevent the logs from being erased, but if this is used in conjunction with Cyber

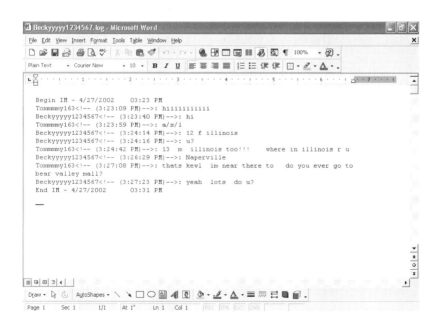

Sentinel, you will receive the warning and screen capture from Cyber Sentinel letting you know of the problem.

When you view the screen capture you will see the screen name of the subject who chatted with your child. Print out the violation and then navigate as explained above and open the file under that screen name.

Now you will be able to read the entire chat or instant message/messenger session and know exactly why the violation occurred. If you need to notify law enforcement, chances of catching the predator go up exponentially. The programs Powertools for AOL and Power Plus for Aim can be found at keyword BPS on America Online or at the Web site *www.bpssoft.com.*

11 How Software Helps Law Enforcement Catch the Online Predator

The six main ways predators communicate with children are:

1. Web sites
2. E-mail
3. Public chat room
4. Private chat room
5. Instant message
6. Instant messenger

The most dangerous area by far is chat.

Remember that all chat programs have private chat rooms, private chatting, and instant messaging of some kind. (Due to the popularity of America Online and their instant message they sometimes receive the blame for everything, when in fact their system was never used.)

If you have a problem, make sure you contact the police immediately, and if possible, note the following:

1. Was your problem with an instant message, instant messenger, or chat room?
2. Who is your Internet service provider?

Most of the calls to our office usually go through a screening process. First we hear from the frantic parents that their child received an instant message threatening to cause harm to their child. When we ask what service provider they have, we are told XYZ service provider, meaning it is not an instant message because they are not using America Online. By asking several follow-up questions, we can identify the ISP used and how to locate the offender.

If we can find the ISP, screen name, and exact time, the chances of catching the predator are extremely high.

However, a typical complaint goes something like this:

PARENT: My child was online chatting last night and this horrible person said he was going to hurt my child.

OFFICER: What was the screen name of the subject that said this to your child?

PARENT: Well, I think his screen name was BADGUY123 or something like that.

OFFICER: What Internet service provider do you use?

PARENT: My child was on one of the two ISPs we have. I

am not sure which one because my child closed the ISP before telling me about the problem.

OFFICER: At what time exactly did this occur?

PARENT: I think the time was maybe seven or eight last night.

As you can see, this leaves law enforcement with almost an insurmountable amount of obstacles. When tracking down offenders on the Internet, we need to be specific— down to the second and in the proper time zone—or we will more than likely not be able to resolve the complaint and identify a subject.

But put Cyber Sentinel on your machine, back it up with Power Tools or Power Plus for AIM, and everything to make identifying the predator easy is automatically recorded by your computer as it is happening.

As your police officers, we want to say to the predator:

"What you did, what you said was recorded in its en- tirety. Got it? You're not as anonymous as you thought. Maybe it is time to crawl back under your rock."

1 2 About McAfee Visual Trace

Another useful tool is McAfee Visual Trace.

If we did not scare the predators enough yet, take a look at this gem.

But first, let's review why people use the computer and the Internet to harm other people:

1. The ease of finding victims

2. The convenience of having the computer right in his own bedroom

3. The ease of committing real harm via the Internet while under the influence of alcohol or drugs. He's at home drinking, he's mad; it takes seconds to rip off a vengeful or harmful e-mail message.

4. The absence of a cooling off period. If it was a handwritten letter by snail mail we have time to write it, rewrite it, and then the cooling off period between finishing the letter and actually getting it to the mailbox.

5. And then there is what I personally believe to be the most important reason, the sense of anonymity. The feeling a predator has when he sits in his bedroom with the door closed and the lights off as he prowls the Internet looking for victims that we will never be able to find him. He knows that using the telephone easily leads to capture, via caller ID.

McAfee has come up with caller ID for the computer called Visual Trace. This program allows anyone to trace down where the instant message/messenger, windows messenger, private chat, private whisper is coming from. This product will allow any parent to capture the information about a predator online and give it to law enforcement. With this information law enforcement can find him. They can trace him right back to the computer in that darkened bedroom.

Let's take a look at just what this program can do.

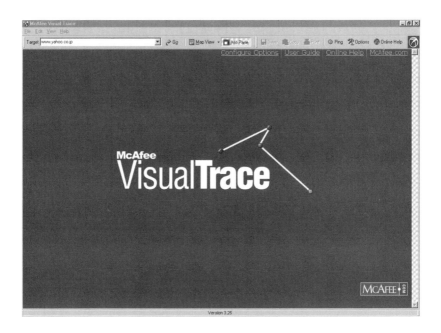

The address used by the offender in the chat, message, or e-mail is put into Visual Trace and within 45 seconds it traces back to the necessary information to find the predator. That's right: 45 seconds.

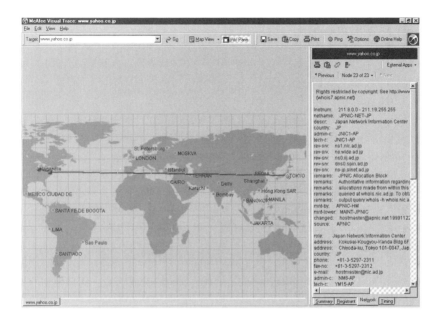

In this example, we are tracing to a regular Web site in Japan. The site is *www.yahoo.co.jp*. This trace took ten seconds to complete and, as you can see, shows all the information needed to identify the user at the specific date and time. When chatting on IRC, or sending files, sending e-mail, or using the peer-to-peer programs, the necessary information to run this sort of trace is being given out by the predators. That's right: he is telling us all this information and this product makes it easy to locate him.

My personal hope is to see this technology integrated with the Cyber Sentinel. What a powerful tool it would make. Not only would it provide the protection for your children, but Visual Trace would activate automatically when needed and do an immediate trace to identify the predator. This would truly be caller ID on your computer. A trial version of Visual Trace is available at *www.mcafee.com*.

1 3 Firewalls

Do I really need a firewall and just what does a firewall do for my computer?

When you use your computer to access the Internet, you use different protocols to communicate. One of the protocols is *hyper text transfer protocol*, or HTTP. Another is *file transfer protocol*, or FTP. To accomplish these communications, the computer uses different *ports* on your computer. Normally, certain types of communication are not accomplished from the same port. For instance HTTP of Internet traffic takes place over port 80, and FTP traffic takes place over port 21. This does not mean that all FTP traffic will occur over port 21. When using programs called FTP clients, software programs that assist you in using file transfer protocol, you may select other ports through which to communicate. There are literally tens of thousands of ports on your computer.

It is not unusual to go into Internet Relay Chat rooms and see people advertising that they have an FTP server up and they are giving you authority to access the server and download songs, images, files, or illegal material from their site. Normally the advertisements take place with an automated message being typed into the chat room. The message usually relates something like:

I have Teenie boppers, tons of pictures and videos at lightning fast speeds! Series (meaning multiple images or pictures of the same subjects), *Web cams* (movies created by people with their own web cams usually in their own bed-room), *professional and amateur—you NAME IT!*

The advertisement would be followed by the name of the FTP site, such as *My File Sever*, and the IP address for that person's computer. When you are online, you use a protocol called *transmission control protocol/internet protocol* (TCP/IP). This protocol actually assigns a numerical identi-fication to your computer during the online session. If you think of your computer as being you and the browser as being the vehicle you use to go places on the Internet, then TCP/IP would be the license plates on your vehicle. The only difference is that with TCP/IP and the type of Internet service provider you use, the license plates can stay the same every time you're online or they may change with every session. If you're part of a large ISP, you are most likely going to be given a new license plate every time you sign on. This is called a *dynamic IP*—it will change with each session. If you use a cable modem, your IP will most likely never change. This is known as a *static IP*.

The name of the FTP site, *My File Server*, would be fol-lowed with a numerical value such as 111.111.11.1. The numbers will be a four-set series of numbers. This is the ac-tual license plate of the vehicle you are looking for. Another way of looking at this value is that this is the Internet tele-phone number of the person you want to call. By telling your browser or FTP client the right Internet telephone number, you can call the computer at that number. It goes a step further with FTP. You need to know the port number over which the communication will take place. In most cases it will be port 21, however the person who sets up the

FTP site can choose other ports to use. Think of the port number as the extension number of the phone you are trying to reach. The main number, 111.111.11.1, is the main switchboard at the company and port 21 is the extension number of Mr. Smith within the company. Normally they will advertise that the FTP site is up at 111.111.11.1 and you need to use port 6969, or 2121, and that you will need to put in a login identification and password. Of course the advertisement gives you this information also. With this information, your computer can connect and communicate with the FTP site over the specified port.

A hacker will use a program to scan all the ports on your computer to see if any of them have been left open. If you are not using a firewall, the ports are not closed or made invisible to people surfing on the Internet. They can come by and try different ports and attempt to enter your computer, unknown to you, via the open ports. Think of this as the burglar at night, walking through a neighborhood trying one door or window after another, looking for that unlocked door or window to gain entry into a house to steal things.

A firewall is basically the locks on the ports. It allows you to decide if you want your computer to allow anyone to enter the computer via the ports. The firewall can work in both directions. It can close all the ports to incoming as well as outgoing traffic. The firewall can also monitor your computer for all traffic in and out and alert you to *spyware* (software that monitors your behaviors on the computer and reports those behaviors back to the company that installed the spyware on your computer). Spyware can be as innocent as software notifying the company that you bought your printer from that your printer is still working. Or it can be reporting all the data you create on your computer to a person in another country.

One such firewall is offered at Mcafee.com.

The Internet can be a dangerous place, with hackers using eavesdropping tools to monitor your PC, employing malicious code to initiate disabling attacks, or running remote control programs that seize control of your PC. See when someone is trying to hack your system and beat them at their own game. With McAfee.com Personal Firewall Plus you can take control of your online security.

Personal Firewall Plus places a barrier between the Internet and your PC, helping to block hackers from accessing your computer. Personal Firewall Plus also gives you the unique ability to track the apparent source of an attack on a world map and obtain detailed identification information on the originating source IP address. Every time your computer is probed or attacked, you get detailed reports and clear follow-up options. Learn what happens to your PC and report hacker activity to conveniently assist law enforcement.

The site will allow you to do a security assessment of your computer. You can connect to the site and click on the links to see how vulnerable your computer is.

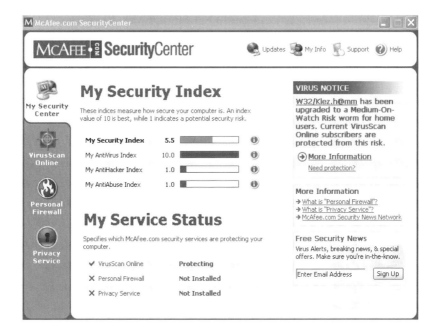

From the site you want to ask for a port scan to see the status of the ports on your computer.

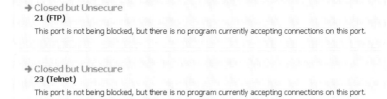

Port Scan
This server will now attempt to open several common ports on your computer. The results of these attempts will be displayed on this page as **Open**, **Closed**, or **Secure**:

- If your firewall is configured to block a port, and it is operating correctly, you will see **Secure** and an event will be logged on your firewall.
- A **Closed** port indicates that the port is reachable but there is no program currently accepting connections there.
- If the port is indicated as **Open** there is an application or service on your computer actively accepting connections.

The time to check each port will range from less than a second up to 20 seconds. Ports which are **Secure** will take the most time.

➔ Closed but Unsecure
21 (FTP)
This port is not being blocked, but there is no program currently accepting connections on this port.

➔ Closed but Unsecure
23 (Telnet)
This port is not being blocked, but there is no program currently accepting connections on this port.

In this case, the computer had the ports blocked and there was no traffic to those ports at the moment.

Another site to find a good firewall is *http://www. zonelabs.com*, home of Zone Alarm, a free firewall for home use. The company sells the full version of the software called Zone Alarm Pro. They offer the free home version in the hopes that if you like the home version you will purchase the full version for your office computers. Zone Alarm is very simple to use. Download and install the program from the home page. After installation, the program walks you through a simple process for setting the configuration for the firewall.

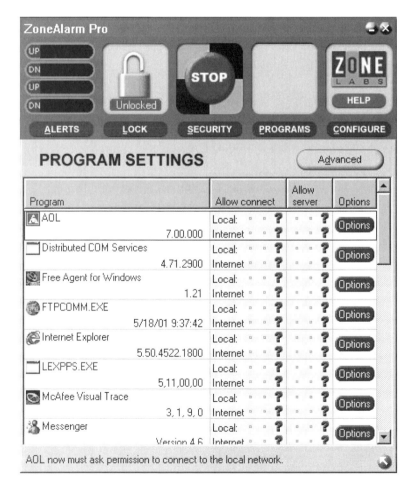

In the panel you can see the configurations for each program used on the computer. First, you see the program listed by name. Then the version of the software is displayed. For example, on the top line we see the program is America Online version 7.0. Next are the settings for accessing a local connection or the Internet. Then we have the choice to allow the program to act as a server, making two-way communication possible. Finally, we see the options button for selecting the configurations.

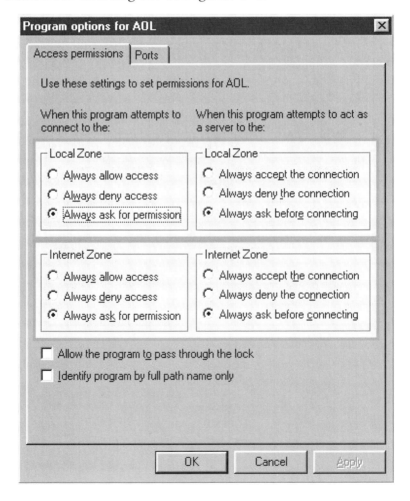

If the program is trusted, say America Online, we can click on the setting *Always Allow Access* for the Local Zone and for the Internet Zone. In this setting, the program will be allowed to access the Internet without first asking our permission to do so. If we set the configuration so that it must ask for permission each time, we would receive the following notification.

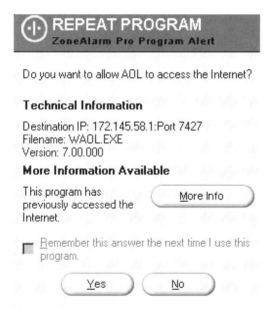

We would have to click on yes, and then we would be asked for our password.

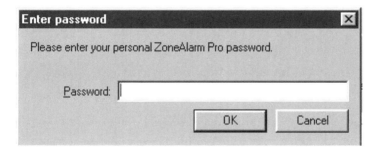

The password would be necessary or the firewall would block access to that program. In this case it would not allow anyone using the computer without knowledge of the password to access the Internet via America Online. In this regard, using the password and the firewall can prevent your children from launching programs you do not want them using on the home computer. Even if they sneak a program from Johnny next door, the program has to go through the firewall, and when the firewall is approached, the child would need the password.

When the firewall is approached by a port scan or someone trying to access your computer via the ports from the outside, the firewall will block the attempt, and can also notify you of the attempt. If you receive a scan, the firewall will display the type of scan, the offending IP number, and can also provide information on the type of scan or entry attempted.

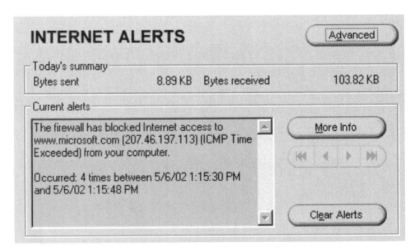

The firewall displays the IP number 207.46.197.113 as the number our computer was attempting to gain access to at Microsoft.com. Was our computer attempting to give away valuable information? If we click on the *More Info* tab, with the Zone Alarm Pro version we can get information on just what type of probe this was.

What we learned here is that our computer was probably just trying to communicate with Microsoft in connection with our windows operating system or Microsoft Office products. This was not a bad thing, and in the case of Windows XP it would be valuable information because this could be an update of the software-taking place.

The firewall allows us control over the actions to and from our computer. If I have a firewall does that mean I will never be hacked? No, there are no guarantees. Remember the example of our burglar trying the doors and windows. If the doors and windows are locked, he will most likely move on to an easier home to enter and steal from. The hacker, after seeing the firewall, may just move on looking for one of the millions of people not using this type of protection.

14 Why Our Best Defense Is Education

Innovative software advances will help mightily, but the solutions in the marketplace would stifle the current threat from predators to a minimum.

I have mentioned before that one of the biggest problems of the Internet is the false sense of security both parents and predators have.

The false sense of security leads predators onto the Internet to find their victims. A false sense of security leads parents to avoid taking the easy and necessary steps to protect their children.

It is amazing to me how many predators are truly unaware of how easy it is to find them. They don't understand the technology, or certainly less so than the people who work diligently at software companies to outwit them. The typical predator receives his computer, Internet connection, and software through his company, a company that intended him to keep in contact with the home office. The predators never receive training in advanced technology.

Their ignorance leads them to flock to the Internet in great numbers. The fact that parents do not have knowledge about simple software solutions leads their children, unprotected, out onto the Internet in great numbers.

The strength of the predators lies in their numbers.

Our defense lies not only in getting the message out to parents and children, but in a mission to educate the predators themselves, because far fewer of them would be trolling online for victims if they knew how easily they are identified and caught by software.

No software is entirely perfectly constructed. In fact, many education professionals have told me that this type of software is not 100% accurate, that it will not catch everything that is dangerous to the children. They have said that it will just catch images, and if the children use codes they will get past the filtering part of the software.

True. But car seats, seat belts, and air bags are not a 100% guarantees of safety. Are we going to stop using them? Of course not.

Talking about the limitations of technology to protect children is dangerous. It lulls parents into that false sense of security, or a false sense that there is nothing they can do other than set the browser controls.

Many parents feel helpless in the face of technology. Because we feel helpless, we avoid taking on the responsibilities that, in other areas of child safety, we are happy to deal with.

Just because it is a pain to remind our kids to wear their helmets when skating, or playing sports, doesn't mean we avoid dealing with it.

Just because our children are sitting at home tapping on the computer doesn't mean they aren't facing an even greater potential danger from the Internet than from falling off a skateboard.

Protecting our children on the Internet is not difficult

once you have mastered the basics of the computer. And as parents we have signed on, from the day our children were born, to an awesome responsibility for their well-being. We have also signed on to teach them, guide them, and watch them as they grow and learn.

That learning and growing will take them onto the Internet. It's inevitable.

As parents, we realize that this is not a perfect world, and doing the best we can is all we can hope for. That is exactly why these three pieces of software are, in my opinion, the best you can do for your children.

Will they be 100% perfect? No.

But they will give you the same peace of mind my wife and I have, knowing that we have done as much as possible to help protect our child. And with the use of the software comes the opening up of a dialogue with your child when mistakes occur. This is the most important part of the use of the software, talking with your children, coming to an understanding with them, and watching them take on responsibility for their actions.

To put it another way, you're guiding them and watching them proudly as they grow up.

4

Active Parenting

What We Will Cover

- The Naperville, Illinois, experience
- The development and use of Microsoft's Safekids
- Using Missing by NetSafe
- Using cookies, history files, and temporary Internet files
- Special note on temporary files and cookies for Mac system users
- Spotting and dealing with problems

Detective Mike's Fourth Law

One determined parent is more than a match for the individual predator.

The best way to guarantee your child's safety online and have peace of mind is to be an active parent in your child's online habits. I know we are all busy with getting the children to school, getting ourselves to work, and then getting the children to soccer, football, piano lessons, and scouting. Then we need to squeeze in dinner, homework, and some quality time for Mom and Dad.

That time can be used to make sure your children are following the rules of the road on the Internet by talking with them and watching as they surf the Internet. Visit some of the sites designed for children and watch as they play the games and have fun. If you don't know any of these sites, look in the reference section of this book for some fun areas to visit. You will also be able to check that your child protection software is doing its job.

1 The Story of Our Efforts in Naperville, Illinois, and How This Book Evolved

In our community, we began to look for ways to help our children online. My partner and I, in conjunction with Illinois Attorney General Jim Ryan's office, came up with a program for the schools in our districts. We developed a program designed to educate children about the dangers of the Internet. We used the concept of Mr. Stranger Danger that children were already learning in school and took the program to the Internet. In school, we observed as children identified the stranger as the man in the car that stops and asks for directions. The stranger was the person who called on the phone asking for Mommy or Daddy when they weren't home. Instead of saying Mommy and Daddy weren't home, the children learned to say that Mommy and Daddy were busy and wanted to know who was calling.

The children knew not to approach the car of a stranger and to run to their home or school and tell their parents or teachers about the subject in the car. *We thought, why not take those well-learned skills and apply them to the Internet?*

We developed an eight-page workbook and a thirty-eight slide PowerPoint presentation. The workbook was created to help educate the teachers about what the presentation was attempting to teach and to let them know what questions they could expect from the children.

Prior to going to the school, we did an informal survey and found out that:

1. Over 65 percent of the students in our school district had been online already. These were children that had been online at home, not just online at school.

2. Sixty percent of the children had already been in chat rooms and private or instant messages. Take into account the recent congressional findings that there are twenty-four million children online in the United States alone.

3. Of those children, one in five has been solicited for sex, and one in four has been sent naked or lewd images.

4. 725,000 children nationwide have been aggressively asked to meet in person for sex.

We were a little surprised at the age of the children. *We surveyed fourth graders.*

We had hoped to tailor the program to join forces with the DARE, VEGA, or GREAT programs taught in the fifth and sixth grades, but were surprised to find that we needed to aim younger to have positive results.

So we decided to take the program to the children of the fourth grade. My partner and I would go to a school and meet in the learning center, library, or auditorium with the students of all the fourth grade classes at that school. Imagine trying to control eighty to one hundred fourth grade students all in one place at one time for an hour! I learned a new respect for grade school teachers.

We would start out by introducing ourselves and fielding the usual questions. "Are you a real police officer?" (we work in plain clothes), "Do you really have a gun?" and "Have you ever shot anyone?" After these questions, we got to ask several questions of the children. We asked them to raise their hand if they have a computer at home. Better than 95 percent would raise their hands when we started in 1998, today it is rare when we do not see one hundred percent of the children raising their hands. Then we would ask where they have their computer, and most would say the computer is in a common area of the house as it is the family computer.

This has changed over the years, and more often the computer is found in the child's bedroom unless the parents have been educated about online safety.

Next we would ask if they had a buddy list and who was on the buddy list. In the beginning it was only friends they knew from school or family. Today it is still mostly school-mates and family, but every now and then we find that some have friends from the Internet. After taking the class, they realize that maybe these friends are not who they thought they were.

One thing was very clear: the children were using the computer, chat rooms, and instant messages in great numbers and for hours on end.

Just to give you an idea of how many instant messages take place, on America Online alone, prior to the real popularity of the instant messenger software being used to allow people from outside America Online to communicate with people inside America Online, there were over 651 million instant messages sent a day. Today there are over 1.1 billion messages per day sent on AOL alone; these numbers should give you a good idea of the volume of messages flying around the Internet and whizzing past your child.

Then we would begin the slide show, and in the show we would first explain about being good Netcitizens. We discussed the right way to obtain software, not to share software illegally, and the proper way to talk online. The use of bad words or saying mean things was not what a good Netcitizen would do. In fourth grade, the children were pretty quick to pick up on proper behavior and understand why only a stupid person or a bad person would use such language.

2 Zoie and Tommy, and SafeKids by Microsoft

When we asked the students about friends on the computer, they would tell us about the friends they met online. As we discussed their chats with these people, we learned that for children it only takes one or two conversations online and the other person is no longer considered a stranger.

The children related that after one or two civil conversations, the person they were chatting with was now their online friend. They let down their guard and discussed personal things with this person. Personal things including their home address, telephone number, what school they attended, and where they liked to play. We realized they were not keeping to the rules of Mr. Stranger Danger and started to believe everything their online friend was telling them.

So we developed Zoie and Tommy. Zoie is a sixth grader and she is chatting online with Tommy. To this day, when I go with the crime prevention unit and watch the program being taught, I am blown away by the reaction of the children.

At first, they listen as Zoie and Tommy begin an online conversation via a private message. Tommy says "Hello" to Zoie and asks Zoie for her age, sex, and home location. Zoie responds and tells Tommy where she lives, her age, and that she is a girl. Well surprise, Tommy lives in the next town over from Zoie! He asks what grade she is in and she tells him the sixth grade. Surprise again, Tommy is also in the sixth grade.

If Tommy had checked Zoie's profile, and I have no doubt he did, he would have seen that she is in the sixth grade, what school she goes to, and what town she lives in.

Zoie made several mistakes when filling out her profile. Tommy probably already knew all this before he started chatting with Zoie.

Zoie did not check Tommy's profile. If she had, she would have seen that Tommy is a forty-year-old man who did not list the next town over as his home. Zoie would have seen that Tommy was lying about something, either in what he said to Zoie online or what he wrote in his profile.

But Zoie did not know to look at the profile and continued to talk with Tommy. Tommy then started to ask more and more questions about where Zoie lived. He wanted to know landmarks such as parks and arcades. Tommy was slowly finding out where Zoie's home was by her answers to these questions.

At this point in class, I ask the children if they realize what Tommy is doing and how he can isolate where Zoie lives by asking these questions. I then demonstrate by having the entire class, all one hundred of them, stand up and face away from me.

I tell them that whenever I say something that does not apply to them they are to sit down.

1. I am a fourth grade student at this school. *No one sits down.*

2. I am in Mrs. Smith's Class. *Two thirds of the class sits down (normally we have three fourth grade classes at each school).*

3. I am a girl. *All the boys sit down.*

4. I am wearing glasses. *Several more sit down.*

5. I have on a green shirt with a pink iguana on the front. *Everyone but one student sits down.*

At this point, all the children realize it took less than five minutes to go from one hundred students to just one.

We then go back to the presentation and Tommy asks Zoie for her home telephone number, and we know what Tommy can do with the telephone number. At this point, a large percentage of the class is yelling at Zoie, screaming out *"DON'T DO IT!"* When Zoie does give Tommy her telephone number, you can hear more than a handful of the children remark, *"STUPID!"*

The presentation goes on to show what Tommy did with Zoie's telephone number, the address, and the map and driving directions. It makes a great impression on the students.

The program was taught in Naperville and we started to get requests to teach the program at surrounding schools, then at schools all over the state, and finally all over the United States. I personally thought this was great. I thought, "I'll teach the presentation in Florida, Louisiana, and California during the winter and in Colorado and New York in the summer." Wrong! Our little department could not handle the expense of travel like this.

We contacted the people at Microsoft and they were on-board instantly, helping to make the program available to people all over the world. We sent them the presentation, workbook, and how we were teaching the program. They created a special background for the presentation. They created a Web site where they would host the presentation and workbook. All of this at no cost. And they went on a step further and put the PowerPoint Viewer on the Web site for free. If your school system does not have Microsoft Office, you can still download the free viewer and use the presentation to teach your children to be safe.

Before long, the presentation had been adopted as the official Internet safety program for several states, was being used in several foreign countries, and had even been translated by one school district administrator into Spanish for use in Spanish-speaking schools.

Today, the program is still available courtesy of the Microsoft Corporation and can be found at *www.microsoft. com/presspass/safekids*. The program is perfect for school districts and for parents wanting to sit down and teach their children about Internet safety. The presentation is in two formats—one without sound and the PowerPoint presentation with full narration.

The entire presentation and workbook are now also part of the home Web page for the City of Naperville and can be downloaded from *www.naperville.il.us/PSafety/Police/ pdsafekids.htm* free of charge. You can download the PowerPoint presentation and workbook and use them to discuss the Internet and safe surfing with your child.

Note: If you would like to use this Internet safety presentation, please feel free to download the program and use it for your town and school district. But learn from our mistakes. The narrated version can be altered, and you may want to take out the items that relate to Naperville, Illinois, and replace them with addresses from your location to make the presentation more interesting to the children in your area.

It's fine to change the telephone number for Zoie, the address for Zoie, and the address for Tommy.

The first time we did this we asked one little boy in the audience for his telephone number. We found his address on the Internet, then got a map of his home and driving directions. Everyone in the class was really impacted by seeing an address close to their own school.

The problem was the little boy did not realize that the bad guy Tommy was me, pretending to be Tommy. He thought that a bad guy now knew where he lived! We decided that Tommy's address would be another police facility. That way, we didn't scare any of the children. After changing the addresses we have not had any more complaints.

In the presentation, Zoie and Tommy appear in the form of an avatar, comic characters, created by the Microsoft Corporation. Tommy is always portrayed with a bag over his head. We did this so that the children would realize they really don't know to whom they are talking online. A stranger is a stranger. *(But be prepared—most of the time the children think Tommy is wearing the bag because he is either really ugly or mean looking.)*

▶ 2.1 Using Missing by Netsafe

Another good program to use with your child is one called Missing, put out by a company named Netsafe out of

British Columbia. The game is a two-CD interactive detective game in which children try to find the missing child. Actors play the child, the predator, and the child's busy father. Through the use of the game, the children learn about the techniques and grooming habits of online predators. They become aware of the type of questions and trickery that predators use and how to avoid becoming a victim. They also enjoy the challenge of trying to find the missing child. In fact, the game is geared so much for the way children think and process information that it is sometimes easier for children to solve the mystery than it is for adults—even adult detectives like myself. We just don't process the information the way children do. By playing the game with your child, you can get a glimpse of how your child thinks, which can help you greatly in communicating with your child on other issues. The program is available for groups, such as school districts.

3 Becoming an Active Parent

There are several things you can do to be an active parent in your child's online activities.

▶ 3.1 Set your online software controls

If you are using Internet Explorer, you can set your browser so it will check sites according to the Recreational Software Advisory Council (RSAC) ratings. In 1994, Senators Lieberman and Kohl introduced legislation to create a ratings system for computer and video games. The technology was put into browsers in 1998 and in 1999 RSAC was incorporated into the Internet Content Ratings Association, an international organization for content rating.

Let's launch Internet Explorer and look at the *Tools* options again.

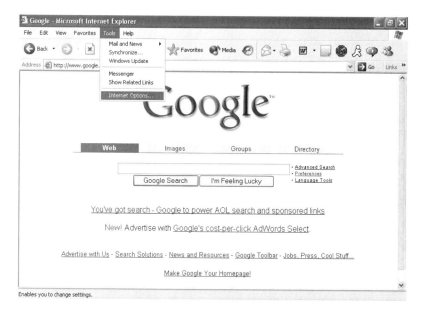

Choose *Options*.

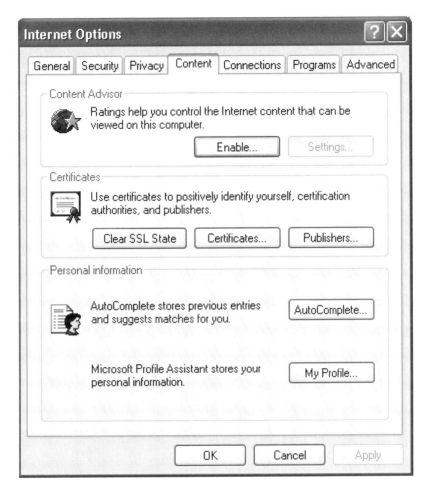

Click on the *Enable* button for the ratings.

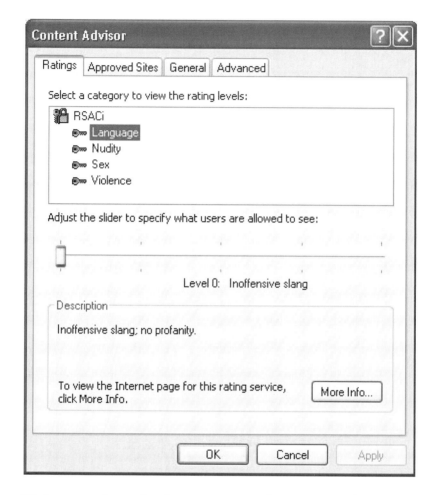

Click on each topic: *Language, Nudity, Sex,* and *Violence* and use the slider button to adjust the settings. You can customize the setting for your family, your child, or yourself.

By using the *Approved Sites* tab you can select the sites that you approve of and let your child surf out to those sites.

These are the Web sites that you are always conformable with your child seeing and visiting often. For Mac users, click on *Explorer* and then *Preferences*.

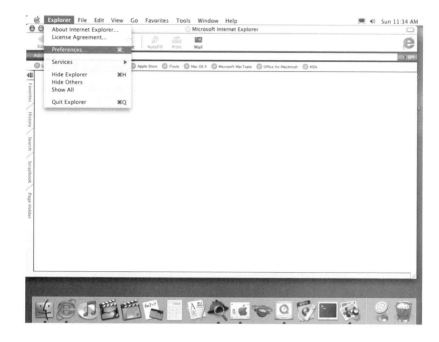

Once that loads, click on *Ratings*.

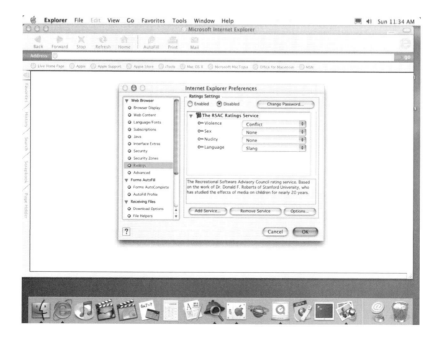

From this page you can select the setting you are comfortable with.

If you are using with America Online, you can go into *Parental Controls* and configure the settings. With America Online, you can select the settings for either a child or different age settings up to adult, with full access. The controls can be individually set for Web surfing, instant messaging, e-mail, and newsgroups. First, click on the *Keyword* button and then type in parental controls.

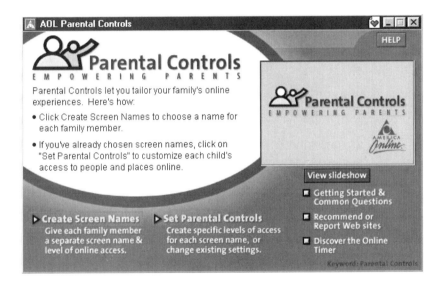

Click on *Set Parental Controls*.

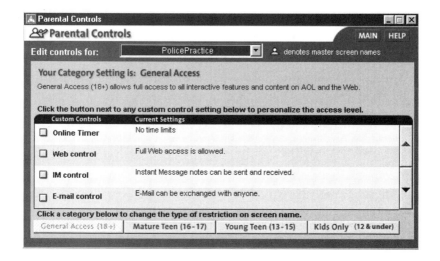

As you can see, there are settings for *General Access* (18+), *Mature Teen* (16–17), *Young Teen* (13–15), and *Kids Only* (12 & under). You can select these types of accounts and the controls will be set to the defaults. Or you can click on the box in front of the type of control you want to set. For instance, let's set the controls for e-mail.

First, you will see the on/off controls.

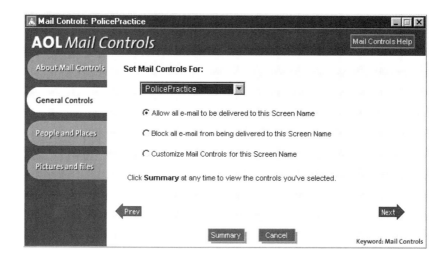

Click on *Customize Mail Controls* and the individual areas you can control will appear.

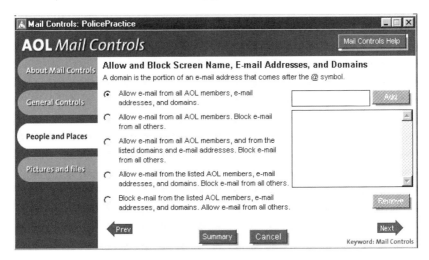

Using these controls, you can allow your child to receive mail from:

1. everyone in AOL and outside AOL.
2. AOL members only.
3. AOL members and specified sites outside of AOL.

By selecting the third option, you can actually set your e-mail so that you can only get e-mail from the address you entered into the box on the right. This is a good way to go. Have your children make a list of all their friends and their e-mail addresses and give the list to you to enter. Type in each address and those will be the only e-mail messages your children will be allowed to read.

If one of your children wants to add another friend, he or she can bring the friend's name and e-mail address to you and you can ask who the new friend is and how they met. Then, if it is someone you want your child corresponding with, you can type in the new name and e-mail address. As a parent, you could use this way of receiving e-mail to cut down on the annoying Spam you receive. The problem with this is that as an adult you cannot receive e-mail from family or work contacts without entering them first.

▶ 3.2 Using cookies, history files, and temporary Internet files

Using the controls, you can store information on your hard drive related to the sites visited, dates and times of the visit, and the images seen during the visit. Whether you are using Netscape Navigator, Microsoft Explorer, or a proprietary browser such as the one used by America Online, information is stored in a similar way. When the browser is used to "surf the 'Net," it sends information about where it's surfed, what it saw, and when it visited the site. By knowing where that information is stored, you can check where your children have been surfing on the Internet.

When the browser is used, it sends information back to several directories on your hard drive that are controlled by your operating system. The files we are concerned with are:

1. Cookies
2. History
3. Temporary Internet Files

In these three directories, we will find the Web addresses, images, and the date and time that our children were surfing. This is sort of a catch all, or electronic monitor, of what our children were doing when we were not there to oversee their activities.

To understand how these files work, we need to back up a step and talk about what they are saving. First, lets talk about *cookies*.

A cookie records information about you and sends that information to your hard drive for later use. Say you visit a Web site that asks you to enter certain information so that when you come back it will remember you and not have to ask for the information again. Most commonly, this is used in Web sites that ask you to sign in and give some information about yourself. The site leaves a cookie on your hard drive so that when you return, it reads the cookie, knows who you are, and lets you back in without having to sign up all over again.

Cookies can also remember what version of software you have and when you visit the home site for that software, let you know that there is a newer version of the software, and inquire whether or not you would like to purchase it.

Having some software company read my hard drive brings George Orwell's book *1984* to mind, but most parents don't mind this feature.

You can look on your hard drive for all the cookies left by your children's surfing. The first thing to know is how to find the cookies and understand what they mean. The first step (for Windows users) is to right click on the *Start* button on the lower left corner of your screen.

Right clicking on the *Start* button will open a second menu. On that menu click on *Explore*.

After clicking on *Explore* you will be able to view the contents of your computer. It will display the various drives and directories. In the first view, you will see the drives associated with your particular computer. In this example you will see the A drive, which is the floppy diskette drive. Our example shows the drives in alphabetical order and in un-expanded format.

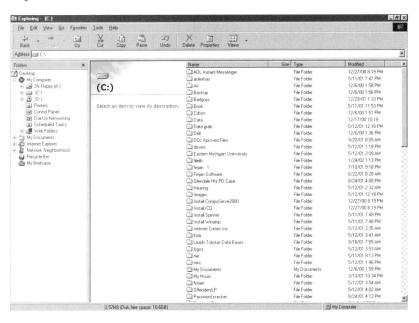

In this example, the drives A, C, and D, along with the Desktop, My Computer, and Recycle Bin can be seen in the left window pane. Because I clicked once on the C drive, which in this example is the hard drive, in the right window pane we can see all the subdirectories contained on the hard drive in the left window pane. Another way to view the subdirectories of the hard drive would be to click on the "+" sign in front of the icon for the C drive. By clicking on the plus sign, the directory expands in the left pane.

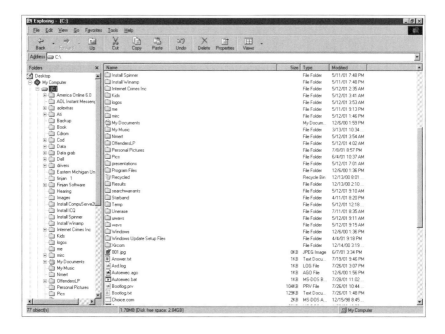

Click on one of the subdirectories in the left window and see the contents of that directory in the right window. Since you want to see Cookies, History, and Temporary Internet Files, click on the Windows subdirectory in the left window and view the contents in the right window.

In some cases, when you click on the Windows sub-directory in the left window you will receive a warning that altering any files in this sub-directory can cause your computer to stop functioning. Ignore this. You are not going to delete any files from this area, so it will not adversely affect your computer.

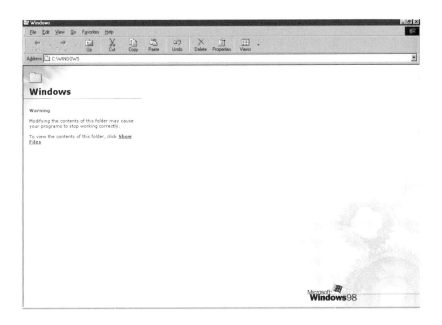

Go ahead and click on *Show All Files* in the right windowpane and you should see something similar to the example below. If you look at the right windowpane you can see the subdirectories, *Cookies* and *History*, and if we were to scroll down, we would see the *Temporary Internet Files* subdirectory.

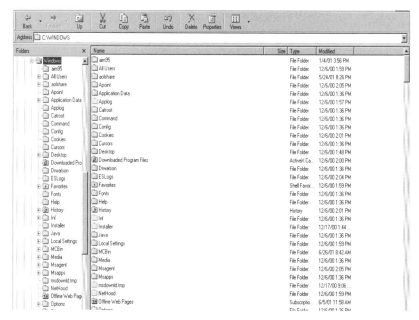

Let's click on the subdirectory *Cookies* to view the actual cookies on the hard drive. In the details view we can see several things about the cookies.

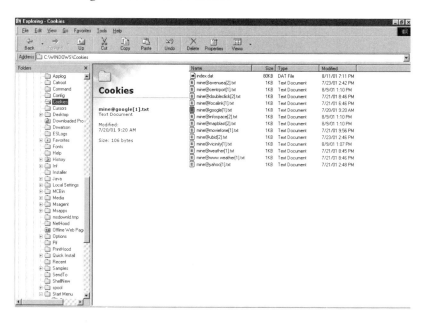

Under the name column you can see the name of the site that put the cookie on your hard drive. In this example, we will look at the cookie from the search engine Google. First we see the cookie by the name, Google. It is a text document and it was last modified at 9:20 A.M on July 20, 2001. Each time your children surf on the Internet and the site sends a cookie, you can see the time, the date, and the site where they surfed.

But if we look at the history file, we can see the actual Web address of the site your child visited.

If you double click on the address in the *History* subdirectory, the computer would open a program to allow you to see some of the information related to the cookie.

In this example, you have learned that your child used the Web site Google (one of the more popular, and easy to use search engines). By visiting the site, you will change the details in *Cookies*, *History*, and *Temporary Internet Files*, as they will reflect your visit as the last time the files were modified. There is another way to view the content your children saw without launching your browser and changing the files on the hard drive.

You can do this by looking in one more subdirectory in the Windows directory. That subdirectory is *Temporary Internet Files*. Every Web page is made up of numerous parts. Many of the parts are graphics that were viewed by your child when he or she visited the Web page. When your child was visiting the Web page, all the images that were viewed on the monitor are now resident on your computer's hard drive. This does not mean that your child actually selected any items to be downloaded to your computer; it only means that the images were viewed.

In the example below you can see the contents of the *Temporary Internet Files* subdirectory displayed.

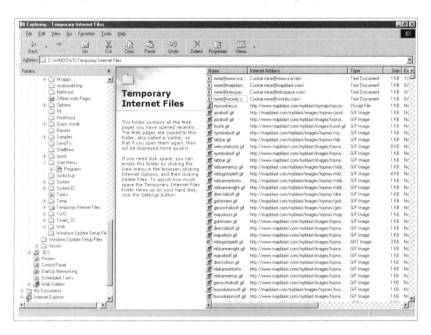

In this example, you see the file marked Google and if you double click on it, Microsoft Explorer will open. In the first case, it is the red letter "o" in the word Google on the search engine's opening page.

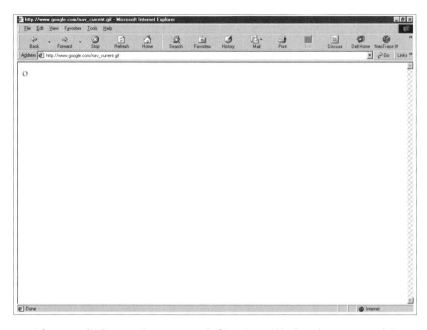

If you click on the second file, it will do the same thing, only this time we will see the yellow "o" in the word Google on the same page.

By clicking on the different files located in the *Temporary Internet Files* subdirectory, you can get an overview of the sites and images your child saw while surfing the Internet.

▶ 3.3 Special note for Mac users on cookies and temporary files

For Mac users, the method of finding these subdirectories is a little different. First, click on the word *File* at the top of the page and then click on *Find*.

The next window you will see is *Sherlock* and you can see the Macintosh HD (hard drive) is shown in the window. Put a check mark in the box to the left of the Mac hard drive. This selects the area *Sherlock* is going to search for the files we want to view.

First we are going to search for cookies. In the search box just above where we selected the Mac hard drive, we are going to type in the word *cookies* and click on the magnifying glass to the right to start the search.

The search has taken us to the cookies. No cookies were resident on this machine because it was new. If the machine had been out to the Internet, you would see the cookies, type, date modified, and size all displayed in this window.

For history files, the usage is a little different again on the Mac. First, go to the search box and type in *history*.

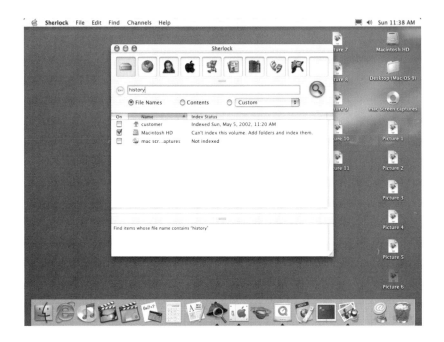

In this view we would see all the files associated with the history of surfing on this machine. Finally, let's find the *Temporary Internet Files* subdirectory. Type in *Temporary Internet Files* in the search box. Then click on the magnifying glass.

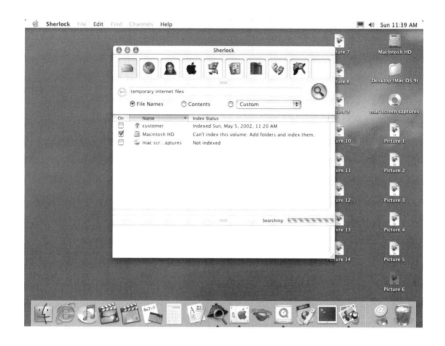

4 | Spotting and Dealing with Problems

If your child is computer literate, he or she may know how to go into the options on your browser and change the settings so that it will automatically delete the files. He or she may come in through Windows Explorer, just like we did, to view the files and delete them. This is where communicating with your child comes into play. In the chapter on software, we looked at how to set the browser, on those pages were also the setting for how long the images and history should remain on your hard drive before being over written by new sites. Also there was a setting for how much of the hard drive should be allocated to saving these types of files. You can go back and check your own machine.

If you notice that every time you go into these subdirectories they are empty, and you have checked the settings and the browser should be saving the files for twenty days and using five to ten percent of the hard drive for the files, you have just learned that your child is computer literate. He or she is removing the files after surfing. It means your child is hiding something from you and needs to be spoken to immediately. Destroying the evidence trail is never a good thing. It may be as simply that your child was tricked into visiting a site and is too embarrassed to tell you. Or it can mean your child has a new online friend who is computer literate and is teaching your child how to destroy the evidence of that online friendship.

Remember, do not overreact, but do react and have a discussion with your child.

PART THREE

Understanding the Computer and the Internet ▶

5

Understanding Your Computer– Computer Basics

OVERVIEW ▶▶

What You Will Learn

- Basic knowledge of your Windows or Macintosh computer.

How You Will Feel

- Less intimidated by the big box on your desk . . . or by third graders who seem to know so much more than we parents do! Ready to learn about the world of software.

What Is Covered

- Choosing your computer
- The basic factors
- Operating systems
- Connectivity
- Files, folders and drives
- A primer on size, storage, and how the computer thinks
- Floppy diskettes
- Zip disks
- Compact disks (CDs)
- JAZ drives
- Saving, and moving files
- Hidden files
- Copying or moving from the disk to the computer
- Finding Files

Detective Mike's Fifth Law

Everything that is digital can be manipulated and everything on a computer is digital.

There is no such thing as a bad computer. There are, however, plenty of bad people, and many of them are well-trained on how to use the Internet to harm you and your children.

But even those with a lot of day-to-day experience with computers at home or at the office do not use them in the same way as their kids. And, the parents of younger children are experiencing issues of safety and security for the first time.

Finally, the world of computers is changing so quickly that the experiences we are familiar with are changing every day.

Over the next few pages, we will begin with the most basic of computer experiences. If you have never even so much as turned a computer on, this section will help you to choose the right equipment for your needs, and for a safe computing experience.

1 Choosing Your Computer

▶ 1.1 Less is more

When purchasing a computer—no matter if it is your first computer or your tenth—make a list of all the activities your family wants to enjoy on the computer and with the online experience.

The basic rule of thumb is to buy the smallest and least expensive computer you can find that can handle your basic needs over the next three years. It is difficult to predict just what your computing needs will be over that time period, but keep in mind that your home system will not be asked to run as many programs, store as much data, and work as hard as your computer at the office. Because of this, you do not need to purchase the top of the line, most fully-equipped, and most expensive computer in the store.

▶ 1.2 The basic factors

All computer brands and models are different, but the basic factors to consider when choosing your new computer are the same: speed, memory, and operating system.

The *speed* of a computer is measured in Hertz units. One million Hertz is a MegaHertz, or 1MHz. A billion Hertz is one Gigahertz, or1 GHz. PCs are available with speeds of up to 2 GHz. Buyers of high-end systems are typically computer enthusiasts, or people who use sophisticated software at home. All computers with 600MHz to 1.6 GHz or better speed are modern enough to support safe family computing.

If your machine is not currently at one of these speeds, it does not mean that you have to go out and buy the newest and fastest model on the market today. The fact is that manufactures of the processor chip in your computer do not agree on how to rate the speed of the processor either. They use different methods for rating the speed of the chips. At work we use machines with 366 MHz and 650 MHz processors and they are more then adequate for surfing on the Internet, chatting, and streaming video.

Even more important than speed is *memory*. There is long-term memory, which determines how many files you can save, and short-term memory (called RAM), which determines how many files and programs you can use at one time.

Memory is expressed in bytes, but typically in units of one million bytes called Megabytes (or Mb). A basic family computer should have 96 to 128 Mb of RAM and 30,000

MB of long-term memory in the hard-drive. Thirty thousand MB is also expressed as 30 Gigabytes (or 30 GB).

As if we didn't have enough abbreviations!

There are plenty of computers on the market with up to 1,000 MB of RAM and 80 GB of memory in the hard drive. And memory is not expensive, so buy as much as you think you can afford. Typically, the RAM is the most important element for a pleasant online experience. The higher the RAM, the better the surfing will be. However, 96 MB to 128 MB is sufficient for home use today. Tomorrow that may change, so with the cost of upgrading the RAM being so low, it maybe wise to upgrade the RAM to 256 MB or 512 MB. When you're buying the computer, ask what it's capability for RAM is and then decide on the proper amount of RAM for your family. Upgrading RAM is as easy as changing a light bulb and can be done at a later time.

If you have decided that you want to upgrade your RAM, there are several easy steps to make sure you get the right RAM chips.

First, look at your owner's manual or the outside of the metal box on your computer. The specification maybe written as sales advertisement on the side of the box or listed in your owner's manual and it will also let you know if you can add a single chip or if the chips need to be added in pairs. If you know you have 64 MB of RAM and the computer can be upgraded to 256 MB of RAM, then you know there is room for additional RAM. One site to help you select the right RAM is *www.crucial.com*. The site will allow you to put in the brand name of your computer and then the model of the computer. The site will then tell you the appropriate RAM chips for your computer and the cost of the chips, including shipping to your home. You can compare the price of the chips to ones you can purchase locally from a retailer near you.

Once you have the RAM chip(s) they will look similar to this.

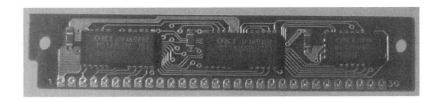

Not all RAM chips look the same, as there are different types of RAM for different types of computers.

Once you have the chip, you want to make sure you are grounded and will not damage the chip with an accidental spark of static electricity. Even this amount of a charge could destroy the chip. Touching the screw in a wall light switch or using a grounding strap will help to discharge the electricity.

Unplug the computer.

Next, remove the metal cover from your computer and look for the socket on the motherboard that will hold your RAM chip. The chip will fit in the socket in one direction only and you will need to either push down on the chip or rock it backward or forward gently so that it will snap into place.

Now replace the cover of the computer, plug it back in, and turn it on. The operating system will automatically detect the additional RAM you have installed.

Memory is one thing that can be upgraded at a later time if the computer has the capabilities to have additional RAM installed. But don't buy less!

▶ 1.3 Operating system

When it comes to operating systems, there are several on the market. The two you will want to consider are Windows and Macintosh (or Mac for short).

Windows is the dominant system in the world, especially in business, and most consumers will be familiar with the Windows system. And if you want to share files between the office and the home, Windows will be your choice. The ability to share is called *compatibility*, a term you will come to know and often hate. You will learn of incompatibility issues between what your system does, what the system that the person sending you data can do, and why you can't see or open the information sent to you!

For most of us, we experience personal computing through PCs and a version of the Windows operating system. However, the Macintosh is used extensively in schools and remains a popular choice for home computer purchases.

Both systems have fans; but for our purposes, it is important to note that there is a vast range of software available for Windows users only. Only the most highly popular software applications are written for Mac and Windows. Mac users can use high-end graphics software where the Mac's technical advantages come into play.

However, Apple is now promoting the Mac as a "digital hub," and touting the undeniable connectivity of the Mac. And when it comes to scanners, digital cameras, web cams, and the rest of a host of devices designed to move graphics and data both on and off the Internet, the Mac may well prove the cyber predator's device of choice. Currently, the trend of the online predator is to use the system given to them by his employer. Since Windows is more frequently used in business, it is currently the OS of choice for the online predator.

The primary advantage of Windows for the home computer user is the massive amount of software available. Virtually every software program for family computing is available in Windows, but far fewer for Mac.

The alert parent will learn both the Windows and Mac system—it is important to be familiar with any system that your kids may encounter.

▶ 1.4 Connectivity

Once you have your system set up, there will be additional devices (called peripherals) you will want to plug into your basic system. These range from the basics like the monitor, keyboard, and mouse which came with your system, to devices like printers, scanners, and digital cameras. All of these will need to plug into the computer somewhere—the places you plug them in are called *ports*.

You will need ports for the monitor, keyboard, and printer, and at least two additional ports.

There are fast ports and slow ports. Just as the computer has a speed, the external cables that connect these devices have a speed.

Choose a fast computer with slow cables, and you will have a slow computing experience. The lowest common denominator rules!

▶ 1.5 The bottom line on a computer system purchase

You'll be happy with 96 MB or more of RAM, 30 GB or more of hard-drive memory, 600 MHz of speed, and a minimum of five ports.

> *Note. This book was created on four different computers, in three states and four countries, using three different operating systems! So no matter what system you choose, as long as you have enough memory and speed, you will be able to communicate safely and effectively with the outside world!*

If you have difficulty reading or seeing a file sent from one operating system to another there are programs available that will translate Windows files to Mac and Mac to Windows.

2 Files, Folders, and Drives

Now, a brief word about how computer files are organized is in order.

All documents—from a basic e-mail to sophisticated software programs—are organized in the basic unit of *files*. A file can be as small as a single character or letter and as large as you can make it.

A *folder* is a collection of files, typically related in subject matter (e.g. Dad's e-mails, or Family Budgets), and is simply like one of those big file folders containing multiple documents in your file cabinet at home. Folders can be empty, hold a single file, or hold as many files as you care to make. Files can be copied to another folder, or moved altogether. Folders can also be locked, which protects them from being accessed except by you, using a password.

A *drive* is a massive storage area with a capacity that varies according to its manufacturer. There are drives with 10 GB of memory on the market. That's enough for 3.3 million standard short e-mails! Drives are very much like the file cabinet itself. And as with a traditional file cabinet setup, you can always purchase additional storage drives. Just in case 3.3 million e-mails isn't quite enough!

It is best to think of your computer as a filing cabinet.

The metal box of the computer is the metal or wood frame for the typical standing filing cabinet. The drawers in the standup filing cabinet are represented by the drives in our computer. We typically have an A drive, which is the floppy diskette drive with removable disks. The next drawer or drive is the C drive, which usually is the hard drive, installed in our computer. Next is the D drive, which is typically the compact disk drive. If we were to install an additional hard drive or an external storage device like a ZIP drive, it would take the appropriate letter for the drive.

When you pull open a drawer for your standup filing cabinet, you see hanging folders with tabs relating what the folder, subfolders, or subdirectories, contain. It is the same on a computer. If you were to open the C drive you, would see *C:/My Documents*. The subdirectory, or hanging folder, is tabbed *My Documents*. With the standup cabinet you would open the hanging folder and see the documents in the folder, maybe letters to a friend or your tax returns. It works the same way with a computer. As we click on *My Documents*, the subdirectory opens and lets us see what documents are contained in this subdirectory.

③ A Primer on Size, Storage, and How the Computer Thinks

I do not want to get to deeply into this, however a grasp of how a computer "thinks" does help to understand size and storage.

First, remember the computer is a digital creature. It uses

electricity to crunch numbers to create the images you see on your monitor. Basically, it uses electrical current.

When the current is on, that registers as a "1." When it is off, that registers as a "0." It's not much different than a light switch in your home. In one position it is off, and the light is off. In the other position it is on, and the light is on.

In this way, the computer can decide if it is looking at a "1" or a "0."

Using what is called the *binary number system*, these "1"s and "0"s can be assembled into information.

Here's how: We start with a single switch, a single "1" or "0," and we call that *a binary digit* because these are the digits in the binary number system. One binary digit is called one *bit* for short. If we had a computer made up of just one "switch," it could contain only these two pieces of information.

But computers are made of zillions of switches, and they work together using, for one example, a *truth table*.

A truth table is a conversion chart for the computer. It understands that when the first switch is on, it represents the letter A. When it is in the off position it represents the letter B. This simple one bit computer is very limited as we can only represent the letters A and B.

When we add a second switch we now have four possible permutations and with our truth table we can represent the letters A, B, C, and D. Now take the on and off positions and translate them into numerical value.

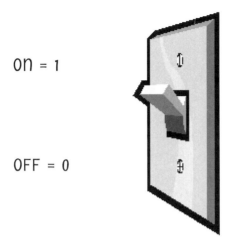

On = 1

OFF = 0

Let's say that if the switch is off then it represents a zero and if it is on it represents a one. With these values and the use of decimals we can translate the entire keyboard into numerical values for each key.

As the computer adds more and more switches, it can create more permutations, and thus represent each key on the keyboard with the proper symbol displayed on the monitor.

In practical terms, it takes eight bits to express a keystroke on your computer. That gives us eight switches with two positions each. There are 2×2×2×2×2×2×2×2 different combinations of eight switches, or 256 combinations. That's enough to handle the input options on your keyboard. *Eight bits is also known as one byte.*

8 BITS=1 BYTE

1 BYTE=1 KEYSTROKE

(One Key depressed on the keyboard)

Let's say I want to spell the word *cat.*

There are three characters in the word cat, so it would take three keystrokes to spell it. The word would use 24 bits (3×8bits) or 3 bytes of space on the hard drive, if I were going to save the word after typing it.

As you create letters, memos, e-mail, and such, each document will have a size value after it is completed. Also, the type of file you want to save has a lot to do with how big it will be. Text documents, letters or memos, are relatively small. However, if you add a graphic (geek speak for pictures and diagrams) the graphic document must be absorbed into the size of the text file. To understand the sizes involved, let's look at the most commonly mentioned terms and what size value those terms have.

8 BITS = 1 BYTE

1000 BYTES = 1 KILOBYTE (KB)

1,000,000 BYTES = 1 MEGABYTE (MB)

1,000,000,000 BYTES = 1 GIGABYTE (GB)

Techie note: One kilobyte is actually 1,024 bytes. One megabyte is actually 1,024 × 1024 or 1,048,576 bytes. And so on. But for simplification we will round off the values.

Why is a graphics file so big? If you look at a newspaper, magazine, or computer or TV screen with a magnifying glass, you will see that the pictures are actually composed of small color dots. The smaller and more crowded these dots are together, the less fuzzy the picture is. A standard color computer with 1000 DPI, or dots per inch, will have 1000 of those little dots for every square inch of space. So you can imagine that a picture that takes up an entire page can have millions of dots and take up a monstrous amount of storage space.

Looking at buying a hard drive, you want to make sure it is big enough to hold all the data (letters, term papers, e-mail, graphics, and any other documents) that you will need to use or create over the next few years. The problem is that you are buying a hard drive today but you are trying to guess the file sizes of tomorrow.

Not so long ago we thought that hard drives of 50 or one 100 MB were huge. This was when the operating systems were not all that large and did not require a lot of the hard drive area for their data. However, the operating systems today are requiring between 200 and 500 MB of space. Because of this, and other technological advancements, hard drives have gotten larger and larger.

Since this book is written mainly for parents, who (unfortunately) will be at least as old as I am, we have some reference points in common we can draw upon to describe how a hard drive works. Think back to the time before music was stored and sold on compact disc, even before it was sold on cassette tapes. Way, way back to the times of dinosaurs, black and white television, and something we referred to as *records*.

Think back to how we would set a record on the record player and put the tone arm on the record. If we wanted to listen to one record after another we would stack them on the spindle and as one record finished playing, the tone arm would swing out of the way and the next record in line would drop down. The tone arm would swing back over the record and set the needle down in the groves again.

This is very similar in nature to how a hard drive works. Inside the case there are numerous platters (like the records stacked on the spindle) that can accept the data we want stored.

The tone arm is called the read-write arm, and it swings over the platters looking for a location of needed information, or for an open space if it is trying to store data. At the end of the arm is a reading head (needle) that writes or reads the data already written to the platters.

However, there is no contact between the head and the platters as there was with the needle and the records. Thus, there is less wear and tear on the platter and you don't end up wearing out your favorite music files from the needle scraping off the vinyl. The more platters put into a hard drive the larger the storage capacity becomes.

The best example of trying to buy a hard drive big enough for the future, but having it filled up quickly, is the case of MP3s. This is a format that compresses sound files in order to transmit songs and recordings over the Internet.

Most MP3 files are between 3 and 10 MB each. The average teenager, using a dial-up modem, collecting 300 songs in a month can completely fill up a hard drive of 20 or 30 GB.

Currently, hard drive sizes are between 20 and 80 GB. This size should serve a normal family for home use, even with teenagers, for the next two or three years. You can also add a second hard drive to your computer for additional storage without having to replace the entire computer.

4 | Additional Ways to Save Data

If you're not up for installing additional drives, let's take a moment here to show you some different ways to save data.

Diskette	Zip Disk	Compact Disk	Jaz Disk
1.44 MB	100 MB or 250 MB	650 MB	1 GB or 2 GB

▶ 4.1 Floppy diskettes

Probably the most common media to save data onto is the *floppy diskette*. The disk inside is quite thin and flexible, hence the name "floppy." The disk around them is made of a hard plastic shell to protect them from the elements. The most common form of diskette is the 1.44 MB disk. Think back to the sizes we discussed. We know that a 1.44MB diskette should hold one million four hundred and forty thousand bytes of data, right?

Almost. To actually use any form of media we have to create what is called a *file allocation table* (FAT). Think of this as the table of contents. It tells the device reading the media what is stored on the media and where it can be found. Because every type of media needs this table of contents, it takes away some of the storage space. So if you can put 1.38 Mb onto a 1.44 Mb floppy you are doing well.

Floppies are cheap. If you buy the diskettes in bulk they will cost you pennies each. Also, almost every computer in use today will come with a floppy disk drive as standard equipment.

▶ 4.2 Zip disks

The next step up in storage media is the *Zip disk*. Think of this as a floppy diskette on steroids. It looks like a floppy disk only twice as thick. Depending on which zip disk you choose, it will hold 100 to 250 million bytes of data. That's 250 MB.

These are very handy items to have. They are great for saving large files, or even more valuable for moving files from one computer to another. The downside to the use of zip disks it that not every computer has a zip drive as standard equipment. However, the drives are not that expensive and are easily installed.

Having one on your work computer, copying files at work to the zip disk, thinking you can work on them at home, and then learning you don't have a zip drive on your home computer is called a *compatibility problem*.

A compatibility problem does not mean the inability to get along with your spouse or children. It is geek speak for, "Does not play well with others, or you cannot do that because my computer does not have that type of drive."

The other consideration when using a zip disk is the cost

of the disks. At the time of this writing, the average price of a zip disk is between $17 and $19 each. The drive itself will cost between $80 and $100. This is in comparison to a floppy disk drive that is already part of the machine you bought and a diskette that costs pennies.

The addition of a zip drive is a handy extra you may fall in love with after several months of using your computer.

▶ 4.3 Compact disks (CDs)

The next step up is to a compact disk. This format allows for 650–700 million bytes to be stored on one disk. That's 600–700 MB. This is about as much information as can be stored on 451 diskettes or two to six zip disks.

If you purchase the blank CDs in bulk, they will cost you about ten cents each. These are much less expensive then a zip disk, although not quite as inexpensive as a diskette. But they're capable of holding huge amounts of data at a relatively inexpensive price.

This is currently the popular format in which teenagers save their favorite music files. Since this is a process where the data is actually burned into the disk it is a less volatile format. A CD is not subject to erasure by exposure to a magnet or other concerns for digital data saved in a magnetic format. You actually have to break the disk or scratch it to destroy the data.

Most computers have a compact disk drive. The downside to this format is that the compact disk writer, or *burner*, is not that common. The prices have been coming down resulting in more and more new machines coming with them as a standard feature.

The actual burner will run between $100 and $250. This is almost a must on any computer today. In fact, in today's models you will find combination drives such as CD-R, CD-RW/DVD. This means the drive can read compact disks, write or rewrite to compact disks and also read or play a Digital Video Disk. You are able to rent a DVD from your local video rental store and watch it play on your computer. This is extremely popular with frequent air travelers. They can play the DVD on their laptop and listen to the movie on headphones without bothering anyone around them.

▶ 4.4 JAZ drives

Going up one more size on the scale brings us to the JAZ drive. The JAZ will hold either one billion bytes or two billion bytes. This is a great format for *backing up* your data.

Backing up means to take all the files you have created on your machine and save them to a storage medium outside of your hard drive. This is done so in the event that if your hard drive crashes, breaks physically, or has a software failure, you still have copies of the files you created.

They can be reloaded on a new hard drive or after the software operating your hard drive has been fixed, back onto your original hard drive. Since you can save 1 to 2 GB of data, you can save all the contents of your hard drive on several JAZ disks.

The downside of the JAZ format is that the JAZ drive

will cost about $300 and the JAZ disks will cost $80–$90 each. However, when compared with the cost of recreating all your data from scratch, against the cost of a JAZ drive, the purchase might be money well spent. Having gone through crashes that could not be repaired, I have learned to love the JAZ drive.

Don't forget for the home computer you received compact disks with your operating system, and installed software. What you might be backing up at home is only the files you created yourself. These may fit on CDs. The cost of the CDs when purchased in bulk (twenty- five, fifty, or one hundred disks at a time) is about ten to twenty cents each.

5 Saving and Moving Files

The next question of course is, "Okay, now that I know where I want to put the file, how do I get it there?" This is called moving, or copying a file. Copying a file means you are putting another copy of the file somewhere. Moving the file means taking the existing copy and placing it somewhere else on the computer. There are numerous ways to do this and one is not necessarily right and the others wrong.

There are numerous ways to do almost everything on a computer; the one you are most comfortable is the right way for you. Let's look at some of the most common ways to move or copy files.

1. Start with a file that is on our desktop. In this case the file is a Microsoft word document, named *practice-file.doc*, and we want to copy the file to a floppy

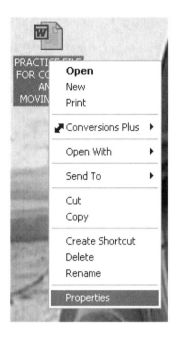
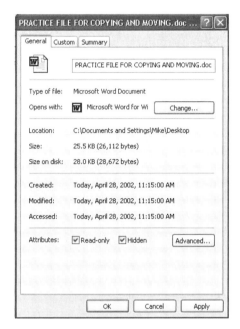

diskette. We know from the section above that a floppy diskette will hold 1.44 MB so we need to check its size. To do this, we will right click on the file, drop down and click on the properties tab, and see that the file is approximately 26 KB (kilobytes). The diskette is capable of holding this file and much more if it does not already contain data.

2. The easiest way to copy this file to the diskette is to right click on the file *practice file for copying and moving.doc* and then come down to the *Send To* tab, and then left click on the *3 1/2 Floppy (A:)* tab.

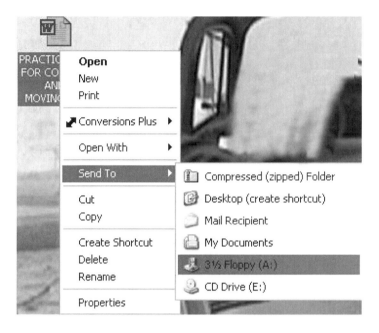

The computer will automatically start copying the file to the diskette and you will see a small box open and give you the status of the copying.

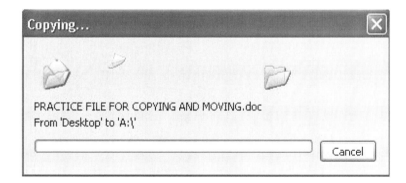

3. If the file is being transferred for a second time, maybe the computer did it so fast that it did not show you a status box. Or if this is an updating of a previ-

ously copied file the computer will warn you that the file is already present on the diskette, the computer will ask if you want to overwrite the existing file on the diskette with the file you are sending. Look at the date the file was created; is it newer or older then the one you are transferring? This will help you decide if you want to overwrite the existing file or not.

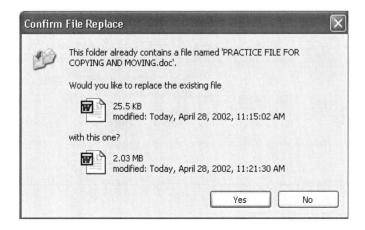

4. Another way to view file types, contents, and sizes, is by changing the views on the tool bar. By changing the views we can obtain different information about the contents of the drive or directory. In the *Icon* view we see large icons telling us what type of program made the file.

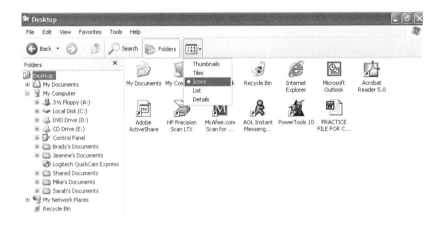

In the *List* view we can see everything in a list, arranged by the name, size, or date of the file on the drive or directory.

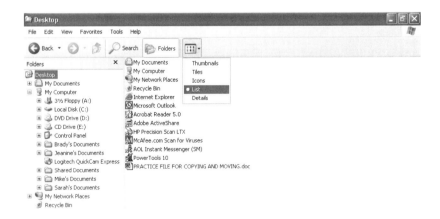

In the *Thumbnail* view we can see what the file actually looks like. If it is a graphic, we see the picture.

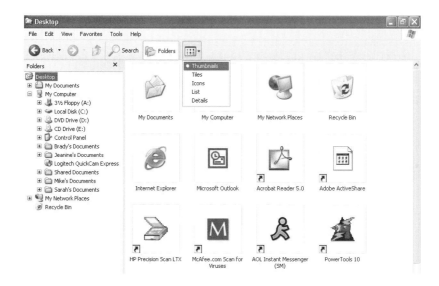

In the *Detail* view we see the details attributed to that file—the name, the size of the file, type of file (the program used to create the file), and the date it was last modified. This view affords us the most information about the file.

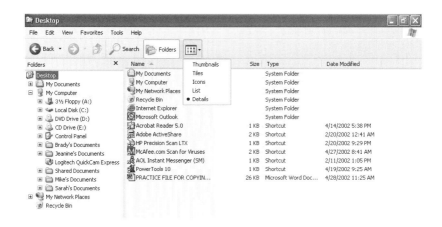

6 Hidden Files

Files that cannot be seen in standard views are called hidden files. Most hidden files have to do with the operation of your computer. They are hidden so that the average computer user does not accidentally alter or delete them and cause his or her computer to stop working properly.

In our example, if we right click on the file, click on the *Properties* tab, and then in the *General* tab go to the bottom. We have the options of making the file a hidden file, or a read only file, or both. If we were to make the file a read only file it would not allow us to make changes to the file.

We can read the file, use the file if it were a slide show, and not accidentally delete anything from the show. To alter the file we would have to come back to the property tabs and uncheck the read only box.

7 Copying or Moving from the Disk to the Computer

If you wish to copy or move something from the diskette to your computer, either to the desktop, or the C drive, or the CD: drive, here's what you do.

1. Right click on the start button on the lower left hand corner of the screen.

2. Allow the window to open, and then click on *Explore*. This is the program Windows Explore and it will let us look at our computer.

In the first window we see the desktop and the different drives on the computer. In this view it really does look like a mini-filing cabinet with all the drawers lined up and closed.

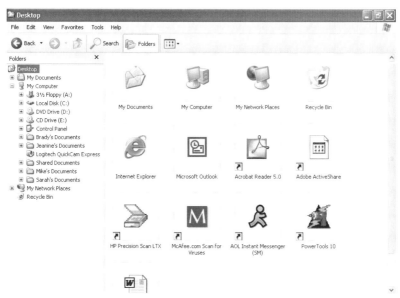

3. Left click on the A drive. We now see the files on the A drive in the window.

4. Click on the file in the right window and drag the file over to and touch it to the drive or subdirectory where we want to copy the file.

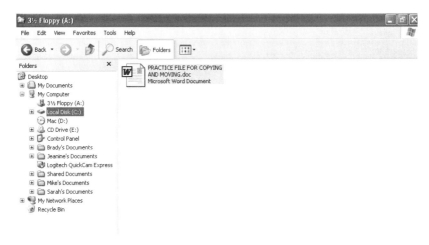

We can expand the other drives and move files from one drive to another.

Keep in mind, copying a file means you are putting another copy of the file somewhere. Moving the file means taking the existing copy and placing somewhere else on the computer.

8 Finding Files

One last handy tool is the *find files tool*. This tool will allow you to search for files on your computer. You know you spent all last night working on that project or paper and then saved it to the hard drive but forgot where on the drive you saved it, or maybe even what you named it. The computer will help you find the file.

First, right click on the start button and go to either *Find* or *Search*, depending on which operating system you are using. Click on *Search* in our example and you will see the search box.

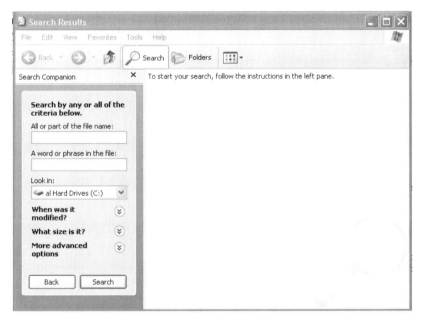

This box allows you to enter in the name of the file that you are searching for and the location where the file can be found. The second box will allow you to type in some of the words you used to create the file and actually read the text in each file. As it finds matches for the text, it will display the results and allow you to select the proper file.

If you cannot remember the name of the file or some of the text of the file, you can search by the date. Click on *When was it modified?*

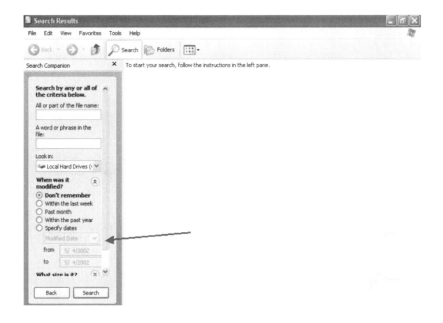

In this box you can enter a time frame when you believe the file was created and ask the computer to display the names of all the files created during that time. Once the file is displayed, you can open it or click on it and hit the delete key to remove the file from being seen.

6

Peripheral Devices

What You'll Learn

- About the usual and unusual devices that plug into your computer

What Is Covered

- Keyboards, mice, and monitors
- Printers
- Scanners
- Modems/DSL
- Cameras
- CDs
- Mobile devices

Detective Mike's Sixth Law

The increase in danger is proportional to the number of devices you have, divided by the time you spend educating your children about them.

Any device that plugs into a computer is a peripheral. Some, like the monitor, keyboard, mouse, and printer, are essential and often sold with the basic system. Here are the basic types of peripherals and notes on safe family computing where they are important.

1 The Essential Peripherals

▶ 1.1 Monitors, Keyboards, and Mice

These are usually sold with family computers and are the primary viewing and input devices. Laptops and Personal Digital Assistants like the Palm V have the viewers (monitors) built in to them. These peripherals are essential and there is no security issue associated with them.

▶ 1.2 Printers

Almost everyone needs a printer, and they come in all shapes and sizes. As with monitors, there are printers for Windows and printers for the Mac.

The trick with printers, from a protection point of view, is that files can be printed and kept in hard-copy form without your knowledge. Illegal images, such as child pornography and illicit information, such as *The Anarchist's Handbook*, can be downloaded and printed out at the touch of a button.

Very few parents have to worry about their children's computing experiences to this extent, but keep in mind a few key points:

1.2.1 Viewing material is rarely a problem in the eyes of the law, but printing can be.

Most police departments in the world would not think of prosecuting a case where someone accidentally views a Web site with illegal material displayed. The fact is that most of us have been the victims of a runaway browser. All of a sudden, two, three, or ten windows we did not ask for, open after clicking on one page, a page we did not ask to see in the first place. The images we viewed are now resident (geek speak for "saved on the hard drive") on our computer.

Does this mean you would be arrested? I doubt it very much. In the twelve years I have worked in computer crimes, I have never seen a case prosecuted in which the evidence was images of this type. The cases I've seen involved extenuating circumstances such as a prior complaint about the subject or that the subject was a registered sex offender. However, once printed out on paper, a hard copy of the image, the potential for prosecution rises.

1.2.2 Printers have memory.

If you *are* concerned about your child's computing activities and there is nothing suspicious on the computer itself, checking the printer memory is another option for you. Your printer manual or the manufacturer's customer service team can outline how to retrieve the information.

2 The Optional Peripherals

▶ 2.1 CD players

Virtually every computer system sold today includes a CD drive—some are faster than others (which is why they are rated 1X, 2X, and up to 24X for those super-fast CD drivers that load files at 24 times faster than standard speed).

Almost everyone can benefit from a CD drive—they offer a highly convenient way to store files, and almost all software sold today comes on CDs.

As with printers, any time you connect a peripheral, you are offering an opportunity for your kids to communicate with the world in new ways. There are good CDs and bad CDs. Be aware of the CDs that are loaded onto your computer.

▶ 2.2 CD-Writers, or CD burners

A newer and popular feature is the CD-R drive, which allows you to read and create CDs. This should present no problem from a safety point of view, since any files "burned" onto a CD are already on your hard-drive. But if you have concerns about your kid's judgment about what is good content and what is not, it's probably a good idea to turn off the CD burner. There's too much of an opportunity to take bad files, music, etc. to other devices at home or a friend's house.

The CD burner and CD can hold vast amounts of information, commonly 650 to 700 MB. With some CD-RWs, you can save information on them, then at a later date you can write to them again and again.

The use of the CD makes it very easy for your child to hide the things he or she is doing from you by putting them on the CD and hiding it under the bed, in the closet, or even mixing it in with the other CDs that came with your computer. If you have a concern about, say, the music your child is listening to, remember that a CD can hold a large number of unsavory MP3 (music) files. We'll talk about MP3s later, but in general be careful about CDs showing up out of nowhere, and of the CD-RW drive in general if you have content issues with your children. It's even easier to store *The Anarchist's Handbook* and links to related Web sites on a CD than it is to print the files out.

▶ 2.3 DVD drives and disks

At the time this book is being written, DVDs are mainly professionally recorded disks used for feature-length movies. The disks are purchased or rented. Currently, DVD burners are just making their way onto the market. However due to the cost of the disk and burners they have not entered the mainstream use. In time they should be like CD-Rs and CD-RWs and the prices will come down and they will become more popular.

▶ 2.4 Modems and Online Connectors

2.4.1 Surfing and downloading

No decision you will make about peripherals will affect you more than the decision to connect, via a peripheral, to the Internet.

The device most families use to connect to the Internet is a modem, a small box that converts information into a signal, which can be transmitted over a standard phone line. Some modems are fast; some are slow.

The reason for the modem and downloading for most families is *homework*. Yes, the dreaded homework that needs to be done, regular daily homework and monthly papers or reports. We used to take our children to the library so that they could complete their assignments. Now we have the Internet, computers, and modems that allow us to access the same information.

However . . .

Your modem is a simple-minded tool. By having the modem, whether it's a dial-up, or Ethernet, or cable, you have for all purposes just removed all the locks on your doors and windows.

It allows your children to surf out to view the information needed for their homework, but it also allows information to come into your home from outside sources. That means not just the information your child wants to see, but also information or chat from individuals and on topics you never meant your children to view.

Keep in mind, all it takes is common sense and active parenting to make the modem one of the most valuable tools in your home. As parents, we still need to check what our children are doing online, what sites they are surfing through, what resources they are examining, and perhaps quoting.

2.4.2 Uploading

Modems can do more than download. They upload as well—they take files from your computer and "mail" them out to the addresses you have specified. They upload your e-mails and your commands as you surf from site to site. They can also upload your entire hard-drive. There are even programs on the market which allow someone to control your entire computer from a remote location. They are used for distance education and training, but of course in the hands of a bad guy and a trusting kid you can imagine the possibilities. Problems are rare and unheard of with kids who have become good Netcitizens. So you can begin to see why so much of the safe online experience begins with good training and communicating with your child. Make sure they understand that if a mistake is made you are not going to explode, or take the computer away from them. They need to know they can come to you and explain what happened without fear of punishment or loss of the computer.

They are being given the responsibility of using the computer; try to give them the respect of being treated like a responsible Netcitizen.

2.4.3 Understanding Modem Speeds

The speed rating refers to how fast the modem can transfer data to and from the Internet. The rating is in kilobits per second (Kbps), and one kilobit is roughly equivalent to 125 words. A modem rated at 28.8 Kbps can transfer roughly 3,500 words per second.

Most families use modems with speeds of 28.8 KBps or 56 KBps. The faster your modem, the less time-lag you will experience when surfing the Internet—but most importantly, high speeds help if you are downloading files from the Internet to your home computer. The type of modem is not the only controlling factor in how fast you will connect to the Internet. The type of line coming out of your house will affect how fast your modem can transmit and receive data. Even a 56 KBps modem cannot work at it upper limits if the phone line can only support 33 KBps.

Just when you thought it couldn't get any more complicated, there are graphic files, or sound files. First, they are much larger, and second, they are described in bytes. A byte is equal to eight bits. Files are usually expressed in kilobytes (1,024 bytes) or megabytes (1,048,576 bytes).

Graphics files can range from a simple web logo at 2 KB to large, high-resolution photographs of 2 MB or more. Sound files can often exceed 100 MB, which is why soft-

A basic comparison of connection speed and costs:

Modem	Speed (in bits per second)	Cost
56k modem	56,000 bps	$25/month
ISDN	128,000 bps	$40.00-75.00/month
DSL	400,000-1,000,000 bps	$40.00-$50.00/month

Be careful and ask what speed you can reasonably expect as the further your home *is from the telephone office the slower the connection will be. Also ask what other pieces of equipment you will need to purchase to make this work.*

T1 Line	1,500,000 bps	$400.00 a month fee
Cable Modem	11,000,000 bits per second	$40.00 a month

Buying your own cable modem, costing about $120, can reduce the monthly cost of the service.

T3 Fiber Optic	45,000,000 bps	Lets not even go there!

ware has appeared on the market to "compress" the files. MP3 is a music compression format.

If you are downloading lots of graphics or sound files or large text files, you will really notice the speed of your modem.

For comparison purposes, the text of this book is roughly 1 MB. Downloading this book with a 28.8 Kbps modem takes roughly 4 minutes, or two minutes with a 56 Kbps modem.

For faster speeds, consider a DSL or cable modem, which can offer downloading at 10–50 times faster than conventional modems. These high-speed connections are especially useful in loading giant files such as software upgrades that, frankly, overwhelm the standard modems.

▶ 2.5 Scanners

We have already covered printers, or how to get information out of the computer and onto paper. Scanners are a fantastic means for reversing the process; that is, turning paper files into computer files. You can scan in text or photos and manipulate the digital files using a variety of software programs, and then send them along to friends or family.

If you want to have this extra device around the house (and be assured you will enjoy all the power a good scanner provides in reducing the size of your hard-copy files), you will want to spend more time educating your family about the responsibilities of transferring files and pictures onto the computer.

Be careful about the use of the scanner as it is like the copying machine at work during the office Christmas party. We all know of individuals that may have had too much "Christmas cheer" and used the copier to copy things they later wished they had not done. The scanner can be used in the same fashion.

It raises one of the biggest headaches of e-mail and the Internet, which is the instant nature of communications. It takes the cooling off period out of our actions. With the computer, e-mail, scanners, and digital file transfers, the cooling off period can be reduced from a day to a few minutes. The potential for misuse is greater. So maybe a rule of only using the scanner with Mom and Dad's help or approval is a good rule.

▶ 2.6 Mobile devices

Nothing you will buy for the home computer will change safety and enjoyment more dramatically than mobile devices. With mobility, you gain freedom and you lose control. Today's mobile world is an exciting, fast-changing environment of new devices, services, and features. It begins with the cell phone, but extends to a variety of devices that communicate back to the home system.

2.6.1 Mobile phones

Today, there is only a fuzzy line dividing the world of computers and the world of telephones. Computers sometimes act like cell phones, and cell phones try to act like computers. With every mobile phone you will need a mobile service provider and service plan. More and more we see people chatting from their mobile phone. The phone allows them to access their online service and then enter into chat rooms or private messaging. The downside to this is cost, as you are charged by the minute for your phone use. Chat conversations usually occur over hours not minutes and in this manner you can see where your child could get lost in his or her chat and run up a substantial phone bill. Also having a cell phone in most schools these days can guarantee your child a one to three day suspension. Most schools have very strict policies about cell phones and pagers inside the school.

2.6.2 Personal Digital Assistants (PDAs)

The personal digital assistant is a fancy phrase for what you may know as the Palm Pilot computer. The Palm Pilot has been retired, and there are a host of handheld devices from Palm, Handspring, Hewlett-Packard, and many other companies. They bring you a host of simple yet essential services such as a calendar and address book. The typical user then downloads a host of software for personal productivity, information, and entertainment.

A key and unique feature of the PDA is its ability to synchronize with the main home computer. By "docking" the PDA in a special cradle and pushing a single "sync" button, the main computer is automatically updated on any changes entered on the PDA. And vice versa. Many users, for instance, download their e-mail into their PDA, type answers when they have a free moment, and then upload the e-mail back into the main computer ready to send.

PDAs are no longer just for high-powered executives. Since they start at less than $200 and have many of the features of traditional computers, they are often used as "entry-level" computer gifts for kids.

If you are considering a PDA, note that there is another key feature of the PDA worth knowing about. PDAs can (and do!) communicate with each other using wireless radio or infrared beams. Users often exchange popular software or business cards. However, it introduces another loss of control and should be a BIG part of your talk with your kids about online safety if you have a PDA they can access. Even if the PDA does not have direct Internet access (and many do, with low-cost service plans), they can be used to store Internet pages, which can be beamed to friends.

As if the problems of infrared are not enough, those devices that are loaded with the new Bluetooth communication system (radio operated rather than short-range infrared), can receive files accidentally from a user.

The bottom line? Unless your kids are super-well educated in online safety, give the PDAs a pass.

▶ 2.7 Digital cameras

Millions of amateur photographers have switched to digital cameras, and it is super easy to take these files and transfer them to the computer via a cable for viewing or transmitting via the Internet.

Be careful!

There may be no more dangerous instrument in terms of online safety than a photo of your young child. This is the currency of the online predator, and these files are, unfortunately, saved and exchanged by "collectors" worldwide.

For years, predators of children would attempt to get images of our children in many different ways. They would look through magazines and newspapers, take photographs as the children played in the park, or use cameras that develop the images instantly, so they would not be found out by film processing employees.

These types of cameras have even been sent via the mail to our children. After gaining a child's confidence online, the predator will send the camera via mail with the request for pictures of the child.

The images may start out innocent enough, but they will continue to include nude images of the child and then sending back the camera so that mom and dad don't find the pictures or the camera.

Sound far-fetched?

Unfortunately, I have seen this technique work all too well and too often in the cases I have investigated. The pressure exerted on the child to maintain the relationship with the predator makes the child believe he or she has to comply or he or she will lose a special friend.

Now with digital cameras or Web cameras the problem is even greater. The child can use the digital camera to take these pictures in a matter of seconds. Also, victimization through the use of Web cameras is on the rise.

The predator gets the child to turn on the camera, or with some of the new operating systems they will automatically recognize the camera as being attached and turn the camera on.

As parents we need to be aware of the different types of software and peripherals that have been connected to our computer and are active.

The predator will turn on his Web camera and allow your child to see him live on camera, even if your child does not have a camera. The predator will then undress and masturbate while your child is watching.

Imagine this if you will: A subject stands on the corner of a busy street in your town and masturbates. What will happen to the subject?

He will be taken into custody by the police and arrested, or taken to a hospital for evaluation.

Yet every day on the Internet there are thousands of people who sit naked at their computers with their Web cams ready, just waiting for someone to notice them. As police officers we are confronted with the cyber world of victimizing children in this fashion, and more.

The online predator is a bold, cunning devil. After showing the child that such an activity is "harmless" and "normal," the predator will now ask the child to do the same thing. Only the child does not realize that the predator is running software that captures or records the images.

After the session with the child ends, the predator goes online with his film, offering it in trade for other such films. The child is then victimized over and over again as the film is traded again and again.

Digital cameras are not just dangerous to children. I have investigated many cases where the digital camera has caused huge problems for adults. In the normal situation two consenting adults agree that they might look pretty good minus their clothes and decide to use a digital camera to record the moment. This is all well and good as long as the two stay friends. However, if they decide to separate under less then friendly circumstances the images created by the digital camera can become more then a problem, they can become a crime.

Images such as these have ended up in very embarrassing places. Imagine the images being placed on your company's Web site, your church's Web page, or e-mailed to thousands of people at your work place. The images are altered so that only the targeted person is visible in the images.

Another use of the pictures is for blackmail, say during divorce proceedings, when one person has control over the images and can use them to blackmail the other person into leaving the marriage with little or none of the mutual property. A good rule of thumb is that whenever you do not have your clothes on there should never be a camera around.

▶ 2.8 iPods

iPods are music devices for the Mac system, which can store up to one thousand songs. Since these can be collected via the Internet and quickly transferred to the iPod, although they have little interest for the online predator, they represent a risk element for the impressionable teen downloading and saving and enhancing graphic musical material.

If you have a concern about your teenager's taste in music—especially if these interests range to violent or explicit material—think twice about the iPod and talk to you child about why they are listening to this type of music. Is he or she simply curious about the music? Is there peer pressure at school? Or is there a true reason for concern because your child is beginning to believe in the songs and the conduct expressed in the lyrics?

Never pass up the chance to talk to your children.

I know I regret the times I missed talking to my children and have enjoyed the times we talk and they help me understand what the world is like and what is *kewl* (proper spelling in the online community). I have also been fortunate to learn from my children just how *old* I am and that being this old is not always a bad thing!

▶ 2.9 802.11 wireless networking

There is perhaps only one wireless computing option which is entirely good news for the concerned parent, and that is the rise in wireless computing in the home using devices such as the Airport marketed by Apple, and using the 802.11 radio protocol.

Most users have a server, and by installing an Air Port card in their computer laptop, they can use the laptop in any part of the house (e.g. on the verandah) without being connected to the main system. The primary appeal for the concerned parent is to provide, instead of an independent connection to the 'Net, a laptop with an 802.11 to the family's main computer. That way, all files pass through the main (e.g. your) computer as they move from your kid's computer to the outside world.

Easier to monitor, easier to manage.

Just as an interesting side note from the law enforcement side, wireless has brought about a new type of theft, theft of Internet service. Most routers for wireless have a receiving range of 800 to 1000 feet. That means if I have a wireless card in my computer, and my neighbor has a wireless router and if he does not change the default settings from the ones supplied by the manufacturer, and my house or apartment is less than 800 to 1000 feet from his router, I can use my wireless card to access his router and his cable high speed

Internet. Is this a crime? Yes, theft of service, in this case theft of Internet Service. Not necessarily a big crime in a suburban neighborhood, but think how many people could be stealing the signal in a large apartment or condominium building. Just another one of the new challenges facing law enforcement brought about by technology.

7

The Online Experience

What Is Covered

- E-mail
- Surfing the Web
- Transactions (e-commerce)
- Streaming
- File sharing
- Live chat
- Choosing your Internet service provider (ISP)
- Browsers
- Setting your ISP and browser controls and preferences

> ## Detective Mike's Seventh Law
> *What matters is not how you control your online experience, but who. Namely, you.*

1 E-mail

First developed in 1971, e-mail has grown to become the single most popular feature driving the growth of the Internet. Billions of messages are traded every day. Primarily these are text messages, but now include video, pictures, sound, and Web pages.

E-mail has become increasingly popular as a marketing channel for companies, and a variety of hucksters purvey pornography, get-rich schemes, health and diet ad items as well as more traditional commerce. Companies send newsletters, and news to their current customers via e-mails, but there is also a vast traffic in unsolicited and usually unsavory e-mail called *spam*.

Spam was named after a sketch from "Monty Python's Flying Circus," and often is as absurd. If you are sending out thousands of unsolicited e-mails about anything from Viagra to vitamins, you are a spammer or a "junk e-mailer.".

One of the most often asked questions is: "Why do I receive spam?"

There are different ways that it can happen:

1. You visited a Web site that collects e-mail addresses and gave or sold it to a junk mail list.

2. You were observed online by someone creating a list of e-mails.

3. You filled out information online and that information, including your e-mail address, was distributed by the site you visited to many other companies as a marketing tool.

The best way to deal with spam is to delete it. Check with your Internet service provider and see if they have tools to help deal with spamming. They may allow you to block the most common sites that originate spam. You may be able to set your mail preferences to only accept mail from people you know.

Here's help from AOL:

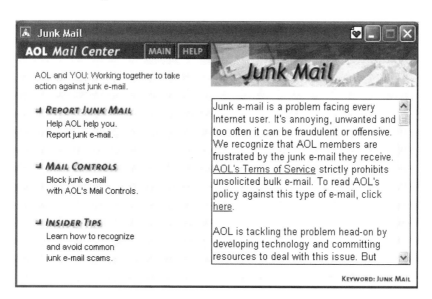

and from Microsoft Outlook:

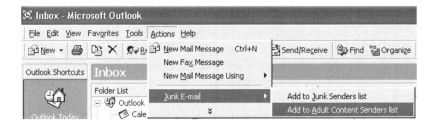

and from MSN Hotmail:

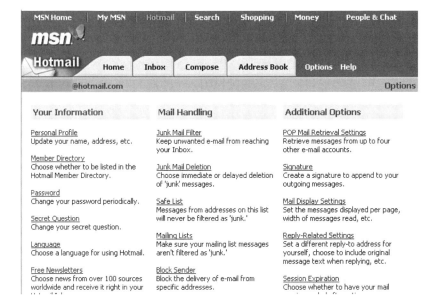

The typical tools are the *white list* and *black list*. You enter the names of people from whom you want to receive mail onto the white list and you enter the names of people from whom you don't want to receive mail onto the black list.

This is a good way to have your child's e-mail preferences set. As they make new friends they can give the e-mail address to you and together you can add them to your child's list of acceptable e-mail.

For adults this can also work, but it will limit you from receiving e-mail from non-listed addresses. However, you will have difficulties shopping online, as you will not typically be able to receive many e-mail confirmations which almost all e-commerce sites require before the items purchased will be shipped.

Nevertheless, using the mail preferences at your Internet service provider and the protective software we will discuss later, you should be able to defeat most of the annoying Spam.

2 Surfing the World Wide Web

WWW does not stand for "Wild, Wild West," but sometimes it feels that way. There are over two million registered domain names and 18.8 million personal Web pages and over 540 million people access them from every country of the world.

Individual Web pages can contain text, pictures, sound files, video clips, items for sale by auction, event broadcasts, and live interaction with other visitors to the site via bulletin boards and live chat rooms.

Sites are created and maintained by large corporations, small companies providing services via the Internet, auction houses, publishers, and individual enthusiasts and hobbyists who post. There is no end to the variety of human experience available via the Web.

There are, for instance, 132,000 web pages with a reference to "Internet safety" and 610,000 pages with a reference to "Mike Sullivan."

To surf the World Wide Web, you need a connection through an Internet service provider (the most popular is AOL), and a Web browser (typically Netscape Communicator, Microsoft Internet Explorer, or AOL's own proprietary browser).

Surfers use their browsers to navigate from site to site by typing in individual Web site addresses such as *www. microsoft.com/presspass/safekids*. They also *bookmark* their favorite sites, storing the Web site address in memory. Bookmarks allow people to return to favorite sites at the click of a button.

The AOL experience brings you into a planned community with supervised chat experiences through AOL Live! and approved web sites organized into sections like Family and Kids.

In these areas, the service provider, in this case America Online, picks or creates the content your child is able to see, similar to online experiences at schools through the Scholastic Network. The children can only see the information that is approved so that they are not bombarded by inappropriate ads, e-mails, or Web sites. They learn how to do research for school projects and do not have to worry about what their requests of search engines will bring.

Let's take a look at an example of what can happen with unrestricted searches, for example, doing a project on planning a family vacation. The child looks for places to see, the cost of the travel, and, of course, fun things to do when the family gets to their destination.

The child might put in the term *water sports*, thinking he or she will be getting information on water skiing, swimming, or sailing. In the school system that is what they will get back as the results of their search. But putting the term *water sports* in a search engine on the Internet outside of the protective community will also get the child information on urination.

Knowing your search engine helps. Search engines like Google give parents several options to help prevent inappropriate material from reaching their children. Google allows you to turn on a safe search filter so that your child does not view mature or sexually-oriented material during the search sessions.

After arriving at the sign-on page click on the preferences link

and select the appropriate filter for your family. This will filter the return of information from the World Wide Web, images, and newsgroups.

Internet service providers such as America Online create entire areas of safe online content for children within their own online communities. They set up areas where children can play games, read articles, interact with other children in a controlled and safe environment. The children do not have to leave the safety of the America Online community to have fun, and parents can choose to not allow the child's account to even access the Internet. See the section on active parenting for further on these controls.

By doing this, it shuts off the chance the children will

stumble into an inappropriate area, and creates more inter-action between the parents and children as when the children need information from the Internet you sit down and use your account, not the child's to access the Internet. To-gether you can help teach your children how to tailor the search words so that they can get back the information they need quicker. In the olden days it would have been nice if our parents had taught us how to use the yellow pages.

Most Internet service providers (ISPs) do not create planned communities. They simply create a fast connection to the Web, and off you go. Each surfer has unlimited, im-mediate, worldwide access to some of the best and worst products of the human imagination. If you go this route it is *imperative* you buy software to help protect your child. Otherwise this type of an account is like leaving a loaded gun in the hands of a child: it is going to go off sooner or later.

3 Transactions

Via online transactions, also known as e-commerce, site vis-itors pay bills, buy new products and services, gain access to private, licensed content, and bid on items via online auctions. As these areas gain in popularity, so does the po-tential for misuse. Not all of the misuse is aimed at your child.

Right now the most commonly committed crime on the Internet is fraud. That's right, fraud. Not child pornography or sexual solicitation of children. It's fraud aimed at our credit cards and our bank accounts. The most commonly reported fraud on the Internet is auction fraud. In law enforcement we sometimes refer to these online auction sites as the world's largest pawn shops or fencing operations. It is not uncommon these days for law enforcement to go onto these sites after large robberies or burglaries in our towns and find the items stolen are being offered for sale online. The investigations usually result in learning the person offering the items for sale has some sort of connection to (relative, ex-roommate) the person who actually committed the theft.

If you're going to buy something online, do a little research into the person selling the items. Do they have a history of sales? What are the results of those sales? Is there a good rating on the subject selling the items? You can also check certain Web sites such as *http://www.traderlist.com/ caution.html* and view this person's site as they try to keep up with complaints about traders by name, state, and country.

I am not saying that this site is factual and accurate at all times, but if you think the deal is too good to be true and you get little red flags popping up (like their e-mail address or screen name are on one of these lists), then look out. It may be a scam.

E-Bay has built a tremendous reputation with a fraud rate that is low. E-Bay also encourages all participants in its online auctions to leave *feedback* about the buyers and sellers they have dealings with. Every E-Bay buyer and seller carries around that history with him or her, and it is plainly on view with every bid or sale.

Online scams come in all shapes and sizes.

There are small scams where your loss will be your pride and the price of a rare Beanie Baby that you pay for which never arrives.

There are large-scale scams such as the Nigerian scam or the 911 letters. In the Nigerian scam you receive an e-mail message from a person purporting to live in Nigeria. The writer explains that he has a huge amount of money in his account, and the government is corrupt or is about to seize his funds and use them for government purposes. The writer wants to send his money to a safe place like the United States. Could you help him?

Sounds strange, but plausible.

He offers to transfer five or ten or thirty million dollars into your bank account and let it sit there for thirty or sixty or ninety days while he arranges for his own accounts in a safe place outside of his corrupt country. He will allow you to keep all the interest earned on the thirty million dollars as it sits in your account for the ninety days. You could earn seven hundred and fifty thousand dollars during that ninety-day period.

What actually happens is once they have your account numbers they set about draining your account, stealing every last cent.

The United States Secret Service and United States Postal Inspectors have set up a taskforce designed to specifically deal with these crimes. They have become experts in dealing with this type of fraud.

Another common fraud is known as the Canadian Lottery Scam. Here's how this one works. You are contacted and informed that you have won the Canadian Lottery and your prize is five million dollars. However, before the prize can be awarded, you must send the money necessary to settle the tax liability for the prize. You need send five hundred or twenty-five hundred or five thousand dollars as soon as possible, and then the prize with be sent to you in its entirety.

The Canadian officials have done such a great job at combating this type of fraud, the scam has now moved into the United States. It is now our turn to get the word out: *when you win a prize you win, you do not pay!* Any liability, tax or otherwise, will be taken out of the amount of the prize awarded.

4 Streaming (Including Sound and Video)

Visitors to a Web site may *stream* video and sound files, if they have streaming software installed (such as the free Real Player from Real Networks). Most of the software for this type of streaming video is free and can be downloaded off the Internet with little or no problem.

In most cases the software will actually tell you what is needed, where to get the software, how to download and install the software, and then do the entire process for you. As I talked about in the section on peripheral devices, this streaming video has created a new means to commit some older crimes against the children.

Let me share an example from my own family experience.

When my daughter left for college I wanted the separation between her and her mother to be less traumatic, so I explained to my daughter how to set up her Web cam and Internet service so she could sign online, use the camera and her microphone on her computer to talk to her mother anytime she wanted.

I knew this would ease her mother's anxiety at her daughter being two states away. Not to mention mine. While I was waiting for my daughter to get her system set up at school I accessed the Internet and went about checking the setting on my own camera and microphone.

I accessed a server, looking for someone else to do a videoconference with to confirm that my setting was correct. On the list I notice a gentleman that listed his name, his age as being fifty years old, that he had a camera and microphone, and that he only accepted *good clean chat.*

I sent a request to initiate a videoconference with the guy and just as the conference began, my wife walked into the room to see how I was doing with the software. At that moment we both observed an image of a male subject in his fifties with his camera pointing from mid-chest to mid-thigh.

The man was nude. He had an erection.

I had to explain to my wife that this idiot was sitting in his room naked just waiting until someone would begin a videoconference session with him so he could masturbate.

Welcome to the Internet.

5 | File Sharing (Including Text, Pictures, Video and Sound Clips, and Programs)

The ease of e-mail and sending attachments has made keeping in touch with old friends so much easier. Sending e-mail takes seconds; sending a handwritten letter takes hours. It makes it very easy to go out to sites find the images you want or need to do homework, assignments, get information on places to visit.

The simplest form of file sharing is the visit to Web sites where images can be viewed or downloaded. For example, in planning a visit to the Florida Keys, many Web surfers would visit a dive shop such as *http://www.pennekamp.com/atlantis/* and view images for Captain Slate's Dive Atlantis. The images of boats, dive tours, and underwater highlights can be downloaded or saved to your hard drive.

With the advent of the programs like Napster, Morpheus, and Limewire file sharing has moved to new levels. Prior to these programs, when we wanted images or MP3 files, we had to visit chat rooms or bulletin boards and ask for help in finding content.

Now, these sites allow us to surf through indexes of content, all downloadable at the click of a mouse. Armed with a speedy modem and a sense of how to use a directory, file transferring is a breeze whether moving files from commercial sites or in exchanges between individual enthusiasts. Programs like Adobe Acrobat make file sharing possible no matter what operating system you use, (Windows, Mac, Palm, Linux, Unix, or whatever). Give the av-

246

erage teenager an 80 GB hard drive, a cable modem running at downloads of up to 11 MB, and they can fill the hard drive with some of the most awful music in just one weekend.

The file sharing does not stop at pictures or music files. Now full-length movies, including brand new releases are available through the file share programs. These programs, also known as *peer-to-peer programs*, allow one user to inquire of everyone else on the system, say like half a million to a million people if they have the movie *Shrek*. If they do, the system will respond by telling the user who is making the inquiry that the movie is available and how long it will take to download the movie. For a movie like *Shrek* it can take six to eight hours, even on a cable or college network system. On a dial up 56 KBps system it can take days.

Once the movie is downloaded it can be viewed on the computer. Most of the movies are not of the best quality and in some you will actually see someone get up and walk in front of the screen. Why? Because they are bootleg copies where someone actually took a digital camcorder into the movie theatre and recorded the movie as it was being watched. Also, some of the movies are ripped (geek speak for taken or copied from DVDs).

Right now on most college campuses these programs are running 24-7 taking up the bulk of the network. The students don't care if it takes eight hours to get the movie. They set their computer in their dorm room to download the movie and head off to class or leave the computer running all night. They are accessing the Internet via the college network, so they are not concerned by online cost, phone bills for a line being tied up for eight hours, or any other concerns a home user would have.

The safeguarding software, the software installed on the tapes and CDs that prevents copying, has not proven to be that successful. The software is hacked quickly and then becomes almost useless.

So, beware of bootlegged copies. They're cheap, but they set a bad example. You certainly don't want, for the savings of a few dollars, to show your kid that bootlegging is okay, right? Our children sometimes don't stop at playing or exchanging copies. They become copiers and distributors: that's illegal, immoral, and leads them right to the wrong side of my desk.

Another problem that has arisen from the peer-to-peer systems is the spread of child pornography. With the peer-to-peer software I can type in the search box that I want to find child pornography or kiddie porn or even illegal kiddie pornography, and the software will go out and find thousands of people that have the pornography on their machines right now for trade.

Insane as that sounds, thousands of people right now have their computers hooked to the Internet and are advertising that they have illegal child pornography. Not only that they have the illegal images. Also, who they are and where they live. This is new technology that law enforcement is just now starting to understand. Technology that is too expensive for most police departments, and so wide spread that the departments working on it cannot ever hope to handle everyone committing the crimes.

6 Live Chat

Selected Internet service providers and Web sites offer live interaction with other visitors through bulletin boards (where text and picture messages may be posted, such as personal ads), or live *chat* in private chat rooms.

Chat rooms are a phenomenon of the Internet age. Millions of people, known primarily by personally-chosen screen names (also called *handles*), and selected personal information posted in an online *profile* chat about shared interests, conduct romances, send offensive messages known as *flames*, exchange picture files known as *pics*, and speak in a polyglot written language combining the spoken language with Internet slang and special characters called *emoticons*.

Chat rooms and e-mail have both led to the deconstruction of the English language. Especially in chat rooms, short cuts are the rule and more and more we see those shortcuts slipping into everyday e-mails at work.

There are chat rooms on any topic that you can think of, and lots you never would have thought up. At any given time there can be hundreds of thousands of chat rooms open. It all depends on where you want to chat as to what you will find. Some service providers, America Online, for example, will not allow the creation of chat rooms that are going to conduct illegal activities. However, others are not so choosy.

Another type of chat room is the private chat room. This is a chat room that does not appear in the list of chat rooms that you can join. It is created by you or anyone else and is meant for a private conversation between the people in the room. Say for example your family has one brother on the east coast, one on the west coast, a daughter in the Midwest, and Grandma and Grandpa live in the Midwest but in a different city than their daughter. We could create a chat room called "our private chat room the smith family 2." Only the people that we told the name of the room could go online and go to private rooms, and then enter the name of the room and join us in the chat room.

It makes it easy for friends to stay in touch. Remember, the entire time you're in the chat room, you're only paying for the local call on a dial-up and not for long distance calls for the Smith family, or it's just part of the monthly cost of the service if you're on a cable modem.

The other format that is also very popular and uses the abbreviated language and symbols is called either a *private message* or *instant message* or *a whisper*. In this format, it is a one-on-one conversation between two people. The only people to see the conversation are the two involved. The conversation is not by design saved at any location and usually can not be brought back up for viewing, short of doing a forensic recovery on one of the computers involved in the conversation.

You can send them an instant message to find out such important things as: did the contracts get signed or sent out, did your travel itinerary arrive, or are you going to go to Becky's or Amanda's party, and what are you going to wear? Later on we will look at instant messages in greater detail.

Unfortunately, it's rare that families set up private chat

rooms for wholesome chit-chat on family topics or instant message each other to catch up on recipes. They are more routinely used for an assortment of activities from the bizarre to the dangerous. Individuals open private chat rooms for mutual masturbatory activities known as *cybersex* and often for the even more dangerous practice of setting up live, offline meetings. This topic is covered in more detail in Part One, "The Online Predator."

7 Choosing Your ISP

While over thirty million families and individuals choose America Online (AOL), there are cheaper services available through other local and national Internet service providers (ISPs).

When looking for an ISP the first and most important thought is, "How technical do I want to be?"

This single question will help you decided what ISP is best for you and how much you are going to spend for the ISP. If your answer is that you are technologically challenged then maybe an ISP like America Online or MSN is the best place for you. They are designed to make it easy for you to get online and enjoy the experience.

They have their own member areas where beginners can feel safe in getting started. You can get information on how to use the service and how to correct errors with your software. In these areas you are less likely to meet with any type of hostility about *newbie* types of questions. Help, in the form of chat rooms filled with helpful techies, is a part of the experience. The people at the help desk at America Online have more patience in dealing with computer questions than I ever had.

However, they combine excellent training with instant access and, typically, directness and politeness. There's help almost everywhere you look on the Internet, but at times, on other services, it's easy to become frustrated. When other users become frustrated with you, you'll know it.

It's time for a word about online hostility. It's out there, and it can be vicious. Vicious, demeaning messages, often aimed at newbies are known as flames. They arrive in your in-box during chat sessions or on bulletin boards when someone is irritated with you, and decides to unload on you in the most obnoxious way they can think of. Flaming is a big waste of time—but the 'Net is a wide, wide world filled with strange, sometimes very strange people.

Just remember that the 'Net is everywhere and everyone and everything all at once. It's part Coney Island, part Times Square, part swanky Fifth Avenue, and part Central Park at night.

If we all got along better, I guess I would be out of a job.

In the end, choosing an ISP is not like getting married. You can sample one for a period of time; America Online will even let you try the service for 1000 hours for free, and then decide if you want to continue using their service for a monthly fee.

Begin at one ISP and move on to another if you don't feel you're getting your money's worth, then move on to another that suits you better. This is America, after all, and the customer is still always right. That's you.

When switching ISPs, especially when going to a smaller one from a giant, look carefully at the connection numbers. This is the number you will be dialing to connect to your Internet service provider, and you do not want to have to call long distance to get online. With the major ISPs you will find they have multiple numbers in your area, and if you travel you will find a dial up number in almost any area. With smaller ISPs you may not have the flexibility in choosing a dial up number.

If you are not strongly motivated to learn the many differences between the thousands of ISPs, by all means sign up for AOL or MSN, which have many outstanding features. Here is a basic table of some of the primary differences between a typical ISP and AOL/MSN when it comes to child protection.

However, remember that there is a slight premium on the cost—typical AOL service runs at $23.95 per month. For some home office workers there are technical reasons related to e-mail services, such as the limit on e-mail size and attachment size, why AOL may not be the right choice for you.

Internet service is available through telephone companies, cable service providers, and thousands of small com-

	AOL/MSN	ISP
Parental controls	Yes but on or off setting only	Some controls depends on ISP
Blocking of sites	Yes	Yes
E-mail blocking	Yes	Some controls depends on ISP
Safe sites	Yes	Not all have safe sites

panies with added features services such as free Web page hosting, added e-mail accounts, or better connections in your local area.

8 Setting Your Browser and ISP Controls

Browsers have come a long way since they were first introduced in 1993, and now they contain several unique features important to your family security. These are your *Preferences* file and your *History* file. We will look at setting the preferences here, and in the chapter on active parenting we will look closer at why we want the preferences set this way.

To set your preferences for Microsoft Internet Explorer, click on Internet Explorer to launch the program. Once the program is loaded click on *Tools*.

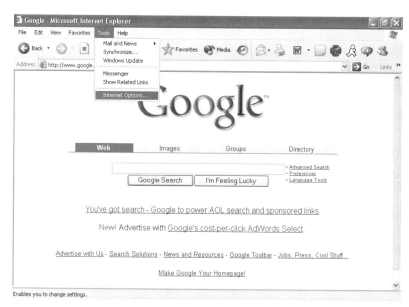

Then drop down and click on *Internet Options*.

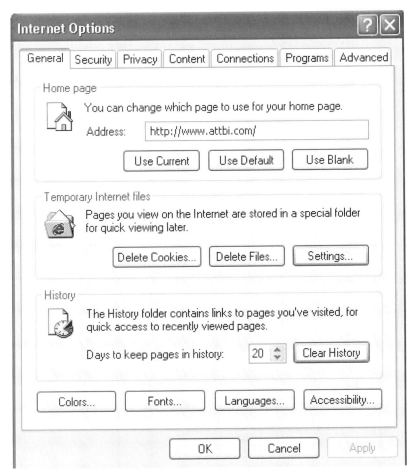

From this *General* tab you can set the home page for your browser. Either select one by typing it in the box, or if you're on the page now, click on use current page or if you want you can return to the one set by the software manufacturer and click on the *Default* button. The next options down deal with deleting cookies. Sometimes these can be a good thing and sometimes not. When you visit a site, it may put a cookie on your machine. Say you visit a site that wants you to fill out some basic information about yourself such as your name and what you want to view when you return. That information is stored in the cookies and read when you return to the site. Instead of typing in all the information again, the cookie is read by the site and welcomes you back. Deleting the cookie may mean you are going to have to fill out the basic information every time you visit the site. By clicking on the *Delete Files* button we will delete all the temporary Internet files. This may not be a good thing and we will look at this in more detail in the "Active Parenting" section.

To set the same type of preferences in Netscape Communicator click on the icon for Netscape Communicator and launch the program. Once the program is open, click on *Edit* and then drop down and click on *Preferences*.

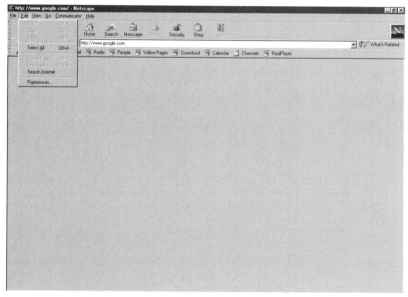

After clicking on the *Preference* tab, you will see the Navigator settings for the home page, again you can type in the home page you want. It may prove to be more useful to have a search engine like Google as your homepage. The search engine will load and allow you or your child to do searches for family vacations or homework.

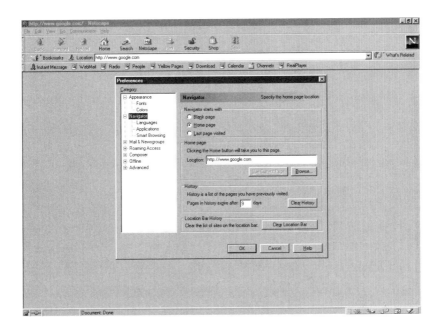

Under the *Homepage* section you will see the *History* section for the browser. You can set how many days you would like for your browser to hold the history of browsing activities on your computer.

Next is the option to clear the location bar, or the URL list of sites your browser has seen. This can show up to the last twenty sites visited. Sometimes as you're typing in a site, the browser fills in the rest of the address for you. This is where it gets that information. It can be a handy reference for reviewing surfing habits.

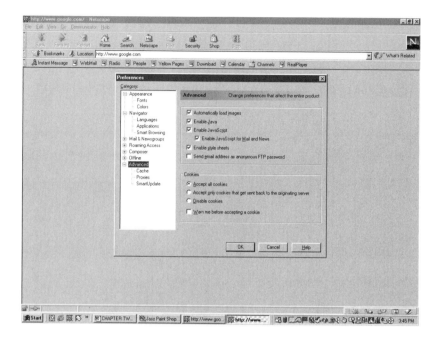

By clicking on the "+" sign to the left of the word *Advanced*, the directory will expand and we have several more options available. First, under the *Advanced* tab is *Cookies*. This will allow you to control the cookies on your machine, or sent to your machine in the future.

By clicking on the *Cache* tab, you will see the options showing how much of your hard drive you want to be used by the program. It will allow you to clear the memory cache and clear the disk cache. This means that it will delete the temporary Internet files from the folders. The same way you did with Internet Explorer.

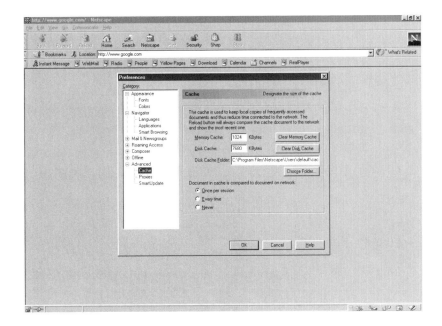

Setting the preferences for America Online is a little different.

First, launch AOL and allow the program to load. On the version you see here, Power Tools is running behind AOL and that is why the browser for AOL looks slightly different. First we are going to click on *My Files* and then down to *Preferences*.

Then, click on the *Preferences* tab.

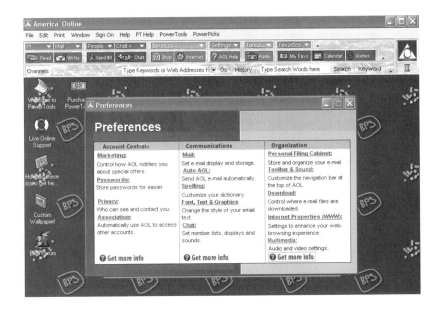

From this preference box we can control many features of AOL. Do not be afraid to look around in this area. Click on several of the highlighted links and learn how you can customize your AOL account. It you need more assistance with any topic just click on the *?Get More Info* link and you will find additional help with setting your preferences.

For those of you using a Mac, the selecting of the preferences is similar.

First, start out by launching Internet Explorer from the desktop.

After the program loads, you want to click on *Explorer* and the *Preferences*.

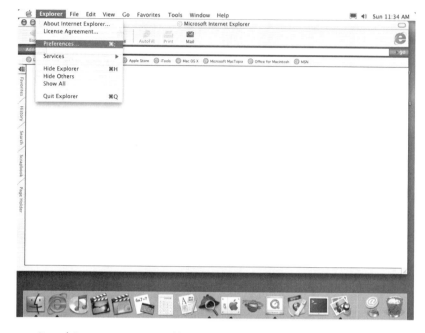

On this page you will see how to select your home page and other valuable setting for Internet Explorer.

These are the basic steps to getting started with your browser. There are more advanced features that we will use to prevent our children from entering inappropriate sites.

8

Software from the Internet

OVERVIEW

What You Will Learn

- Basic information about obtaining and managing software obtained through the Internet in a safe and secure manner.

How You Will Feel

- Confident in your knowledge of the potential problems for yourself and your children both online and offline.

What Is Covered

- Types of software available from the Internet, downloadable or in CD format
- Upgrades, replacements, plug-ins, and players
- Pay-to-play
- Trial version
- Shareware
- Freeware
- Public domain software
- File management
- CDs
- Downloads

Detective Mike's Eighth Law

*Treat your connection to the Internet like the
door to your child's bedroom,
and watch the traffic accordingly.*

---

1 Downloads

The wild, wild west of software is downloadable programs. Approach these with a high degree of caution and awareness.

Always know what is going onto your computer by personally supervising any software downloads and installations in the family home.

The world of downloadable software is, broadly speaking, highly legitimate. A huge array of entertainment, education, and utilities is available for downloading from reputable sites such as *www.tucows.com*, *www.cnet.com*, or *www.pcworld.com*. Communications, personal productivity, and graphics software is available, primarily for Windows, but also for other operating systems—so look out for Windows, Mac, Linux, or Unix versions and make sure you are getting the right version!

Also, make sure you are downloading these programs from reputable sites such as the ones listed above. You want to make sure the sites are only loading and sharing programs in a legal manner and that the programs have been checked and are virus free. This is very important when downloading a program. Since the program will have an executable (.exe) file of some sort, a file to tell the program to run, your virus protection software or firewall may not allow the program to download. These protections see an executable file as a danger and try to protect you from accidentally downloading a virus. To get the program you want, you may have to disable your firewall settings or virus software, or tell the program to download even though your virus protections is telling you that it is not a good idea to download the program. If you are on a reputable site and you know what program you are downloading, say Adobe Reader, then it should be alright to tell the virus software to allow the download.

However, if you are not sure where the file is coming from, if you do not know for sure what you are getting, listen to your virus protection software and **do not download the file**. There are software programs called *Trojan horses* that can cause major problems on your system.

One such program is called the Sub-level Seven program. This Trojan horse allows another user to remotely view all the data on your machine from his or her home or office machine.

The first time I ran across one was when I received a case in which a woman thought her computer was possessed—it would type on its own and open and close files and programs without her manipulating the keyboard or mouse. Of course, at first you can imagine what I was thinking; I thought she was a couple of cards short of a full deck.

Until I got there and saw the same things. Then I learned about the Sub-level Seven virus that allows another user to take remote control access of the keyboard and input commands to the victim machine. It was as if the machine did have a mind of its own as another person far away, via use of the Internet, was actually controlling the computer. There are software solutions to help you identify these types of programs and problems on your machine. The software will not only identify the Trojans, but it will help you remove the offending programs from your machine.

There are six types of software and files available for download.

▶ 1.1 Upgrades, replacements, and players

Low-risk. Players are typically programs like RealPlayer and Acrobat Reader that allow you to view files created on proprietary software like Real Networks audio streaming software and Adobe Acrobat. The company makes its money by selling the software used to create the files, and gives you the reader for free.

The first time you download a file with the extension .pdf and attempt to view the file you may get the notification that your system does not know what type of file this is and is now asking you what program you would like to use to open the file.

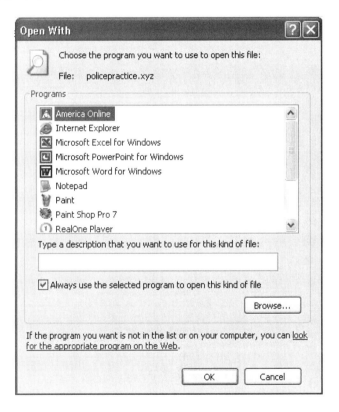

You need to select which one of the programs in the list provided would be the proper program to use to open the file. The view shown is from Windows XP, but the box is similar to the box viewed in any version of the Windows operating system. Normally all you get is this box, and for most of us the first few times we get this box we are lost. We do not know which program should open the file and the box just confuses us more. Normally, the computer can tell by the extension on the file what program created the file. The extension is the three letters to the right of the . such as test paper.doc. The .doc tells the computer that the file is a Microsoft Word file and then uses Microsoft Word to open the file.

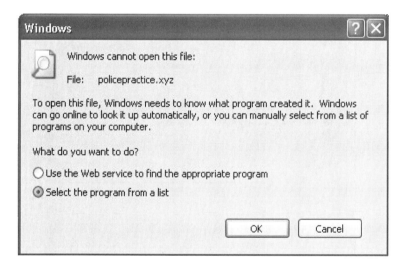

In Windows XP, you now get this box first, explaining why the file did not open and asking you what you would like to do. The options are to let the computer go out to the Web to try to find the right program, or to select the program to open the file from the programs on your computer.

You will have to go to one of the sites listed above and put in the search box Adobe Reader or Adobe Acrobat and the site will show you where you can download, legally, the free reader for the program. The same pertains to Real Networks software. Or a Flash player, if you are accessing sites which are partially written with Flash.

Players are read/play only. You will not be able to write or record. To do that, you will need the full program.

Also, replacement software and upgrades from reputable companies are widely available for free. For instance, you can find new upgraded versions of your Internet browser or the software you have previously purchased in a store or online.

▶ 1.2 Pay-to-play

Mid-risk. This is software which is distributed online and which you have to pay for. The companies usually have to be well known in their field in order to charge up front, which is why the risk is usually low. But never download software and install it on your computer without knowing the company or individual. No matter whether you paid or not.

▶ 1.3 Trial version

Mid-risk. These versions are programs which expire after a limited usage such as "500 free hours" or "30 day free trial", after which you are required to make a purchase.

▶ 1.4 Shareware

High-risk. This software is available for a free trial, and you will be asked to make a voluntary payment if you continue to use it. If you are a Mac user and often receive .Zip compressed files from your Windows-using friends, you will probably be using ZipIt shareware to unzip the compressed files. Typically, these are harmless programs, such as a chat program, distributed by small entrepreneurs.

It is important not only to be careful in downloading and installing these, but monitor their use. With some programs, the dangers do not disappear with a successful installation. Sometimes the danger is just beginning.

▶ 1.5 Freeware

High-risk. Freeware is available for free, but there are restrictions on re-distribution and re-sale. Most of the chat and messaging programs your child uses are freeware and are easy to locate and install on your computer.

▶ 1.6 Public domain

High-risk. This is software that can be freely downloaded, distributed, or sold without payment or restriction.

② File Management

▶ 2.1 CDs

One of the problems of the CD, of course, is that once it is out of the box, all CDs look alike, and you can't easily tell a backup copy of a friendly Barney CD from a pirated version of Death Destroyers of the Universe. Make sure that *you* are in change of the CD library, and that all disks are marked. CDs can quickly become as unorganized as VHS tapes for the VCR. Labeling the disk is not that difficult or expensive. Programs like CD Stamper or Adaptec CD Creator will walk you through the installation and use of the software, including formatting your printer to print on the proper label sheets for the CD labels.

▶ 2.2 Downloads

Personally supervise all installations of downloaded software, and install all these software programs to a single folder reserved for that purpose.

Make it a rule that if your children want to add a program to the computer they must discuss it with you first. Ask them what the program is for and why it is necessary to get it. Can one of the programs already on the computer handle the job the new program will do? If you agree that the new program is needed, check and see if it is a trial version, shareware, or freeware. Explain to your children that stealing software does hurt people and may even end up hurting them.

Let's say your child likes a version of a computer game. By paying for the software the company makes enough money to pay their employees, the cost of running the business, and makes a profit to stay in business developing new games. That way there may be a version two of the game your child likes in the future. However, if everyone just steals the software, or friends buy one copy and then install that copy onto ten or twenty classmates' machines the company will not make enough money to stay in business.

The company will not be able to pay for development of other games or to pay their current employees. The results are the company will have to dismiss the employees and in the end stop making games. The real victim is your child, losing out on new and better games and software.

I was teaching at a software company, just shortly after this phenomenon hit that company. In speaking with the management for the company, I discovered that they had to lay off about two hundred employees due to the loss in revenues because of the downturn in business. When times were good and the software was selling well, the company could absorb the losses from pirated and stolen software. However, when times became tight the company could not overcome the loss in revenue due to stolen and pirated software and was forced into the layoffs.

The management then related something that I will never forget. They told me that if they had received just one dollar for every piece of stolen or pirated software from their company to date, they never would have had to lay off anyone.

When you stand inside a small company, seeing the vacant desks and empty hallways at lunchtime, you realize the true impact of stolen software. It is not just big companies that are the victims and losing revenue; it is talented, creative people losing jobs, and families losing breadwinners.

When you talk with your children they can understand these concepts if they realize it would be like mom or dad losing their job and the kind of impact that would have on their world.

PART FOUR

Further Resources ▶

9

Further Resources

What Is Covered

- AOL special safe areas
- MSN special safe areas
- Other sites for children to visit in safety
- Sites that can help parents to report crimes committed on the Internet
- Information on training programs and sites that can help police officers gain the knowledge and expertise to investigate crimes committed using a computer and the Internet

1 America Online

We have seen how to set the parental controls on America Online and how to use Cyber Sentinel and Powertools to further protect our children. But on America Online there is a special area for children only, areas where the children can find fun and exciting content in safety. They have special rules about what the children can and cannot say or post.

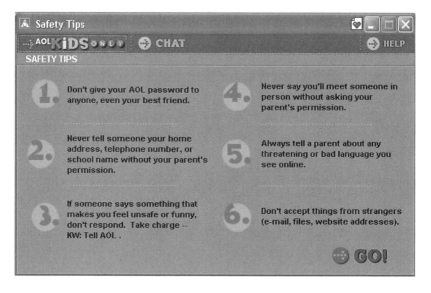

In this area, they take the extra step and make sure that the children do not give out personal information or use more than just their screen name. The area is also set up with different types of entertainment for children. They can check out different chats, games, information, and news.

As the children go from area to area, they are not only entertaining themselves, but they are learning valuable skills. The use of the computer in such a constructive manner is of tremendous value to your child. Let's look at the way the *Children's Message Boards* have been set up. First, the child selects the message board area.

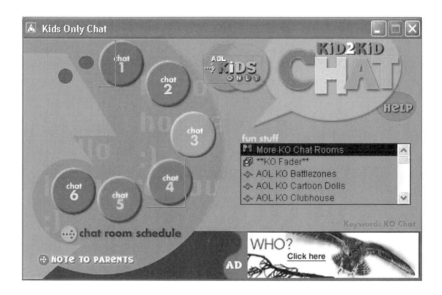

Then child selects the type of message board he or she would like to enter.

From here, your child can see the actual postings and interact with other children via posts to the message board. In the example we have selected, you are seeing the Harry Potter message board.

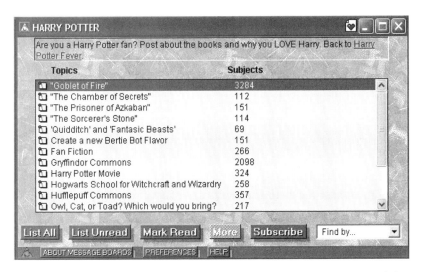

The messages all have to do with Harry Potter and his endeavors to become a wizard. To your child, this is all fun and interesting. However, if you have ever done research for a term paper, a work project, or any other in-depth project, you may recognize what the Harry Potter message board is. It is a newsgroup, that area of the Internet that contents millions and millions of documents and research results. By using the search engine you can navigate to the newsgroups and obtain the data needed for your project. Well, here at AOL they have used the same mechanics but in an environment secured within their area. They have the children actually go through the steps they will need to do later in life for school papers. Yet the children are willingly doing the steps here while having fun. As they click and type they are learning how to navigate, send information to a group and retrieve information on the topics they find interesting.

They can also chat in this environment if they care to do so or use instant messages. Both are handy tools for today's office. In my daily routine I play less and less phone tag due to instant messages and e-mail. I see a needed contact sign online in my buddy list and send them an instant message, get the answers I need to the problems confronting me and get on with the project. Our children do these things and think of them as fun. Gee Dad, you get to play on the computer all day long. I wish I could do that.

Along with their own areas for children, America Online has entered into partnerships with other companies—Nickelodeon, PBS for Kids, *TIME for Kids*, and *Sports Illustrated for Kids*—to provide more content for kids.

Try surfing around inside America Online for a while pretending you're a child. You will be amazed at all the things your child can learn. To find most of the sites simply type in the keyword *Kids Only* and follow the links. Take time to read the notes to parents and understand the type of content your child will be viewing. Also try typing in Kids Partners and see the list of other sites working with America Online to bring good clean content to your child.

2 MSN

The site, located at *www.msn.staysafeonline.com*, uses a cartoon presentation starring Shaquille O'Neal to teach children the rules for online safety.

The presentation allows your child to work along and learn the rules for online safety. The presentation relates just what type of conduct can be dangerous. The program then runs through a review section asking your child questions about Internet safety. After answering each question, a character comes on and tells your child what the correct answer is and why it's the correct answer. If your child misses one of the questions, there is a quick review of what the right answer should be and the question is asked again. After viewing the presentation and passing the review segment, your child can receive a Stay Safe Online Certificate. Here is my certificate (although I am not going to tell you how many questions I got wrong on the review).

By visiting *www.msn.com/kids*, your children can navigate through a host of games, entertainment, and arts and activities that are guaranteed to keep them busy for hours. The site is mainly for younger children, under nine years of age, but there is another site at *www.msn.com/kidz* for children ten to twelve years of age. The content is aimed at appropriate age groups with safe surfing always a constant reminder. There is even a link at the bottom of the page to take you to Stay Safe Online. The site also warns the children about the use of cookies and why they are being used—they help speed the play along by remembering information about the child and the game last played. By remembering what items in the game have been collected and allowing the child to resume play instead of starting over each time.

Privacy and Safety on MSN Kids Web sites

Information for kids | Information for Parents

Are you a kid ?

- Microsoft has created a special home on MSN just for kids ages 12 and under: the Web sites MSN Kids (for kids 9 and under) and MSN Kidz (for kids 10-12). At these sites you will find stories, games and other fun stuff just for you!

- Right now there is no place on MSN Kids or MSN Kidz where you need to enter personal information about yourself, like your name, age, e-mail address, telephone number or address.

- In the future, we may add new stuff where you will have to type in some personal information before you can use it (for example, to sign up for a newsletter, post a message on a bulletin board, or send an online greeting card). When that happens, we will update this page with instructions on how you can get your parents' permission to use the new stuff on the Web site.

- The first time you visit the MSN Kids Web sites, we will ask you to pick either MSN Kids or MSN Kidz (whichever one looks most fun to you). We will store your choice in a "cookie," which is a small file saved on your computer. The next time you come back to MSN, this cookie will tell us which site you picked so that we can send you straight there. We can't get any personal information -- like your name, age or e-mail address -- from this cookie. If you don't want to have a cookie, ask your parents to help you to "turn off cookies" in your Web browser. If you don't accept cookies, then the next time you come to MSN Kids, we'll ask you which site you want to visit.

These two sites are just an example of all the content Microsoft provides and to list them all would take to long. Your children can literally spend hours online in good clean areas, learning, chatting, and playing games. This is the reason for the computer at home. The reason for wanting your children online.

3 Club Tech

Microsoft donates millions and millions of dollars to the education of children—some in the form of the Web sites, some in the form of programs to benefit our children. One outstanding program is the *Club Tech* program run in conjunction with the Boys and Girls Club of America. Microsoft donated $100 million to this program that will integrate technology in every aspect of the club, from actual management of the club to education, character enhancement, and leadership development for over three million children. You can visit the site *at www.bgca.org/programs/specialized.asp.*

4 Anytime Anywhere Learning Laptop Program

This program allows over a quarter of a million student and teachers in the United States to use Windows based notebook computers as personal learning tools. The program will include the United Kingdom, Australia, Belgium, South Africa and Canada. Check out this program's site at *http://microsoft.com/education/?ID+laptopLearning.*

This sharing of technology is something I have seen first hand. In 1999 and 2000 I was on staff at the College of DuPage in Glen Ellyn, Illinois, when we were just beginning to introduce technology to police officers. We used a computer lab, the Internet, and faculty from the college to teach technology to law enforcement officials. At this time I called Microsoft and explained what we were attempting to do, and they provided the funds to supply two classrooms filled with computer work stations, fifty-one in all, for use in training police officers (see *http://www.microsoft.com/PressPass/features/2000/03-20crimelab.asp*). The computers are used to teach investigation of crimes committed using computers: "Policing the Youth on the Internet" and "The Internet and the Law." For a full description of classes available to law enforcement officials see *http://www.cod.edu/slea/continuing_ed.htm.*

▶ 4.1 The National Center for Missing and Exploited Children

The Web site *www.ncmec.org* is full of helpful tips and literature for parents and children. In fact, most of the handouts you see today concerning being safe online probably got the basis from one or more of the documents created at the National Center. Almost every pamphlet that followed in one way or another restated the original warnings or carried on the same message to protect children.

By clicking on the *Education and Resource* tab you will be taken to the section dealing with ongoing classes and written literature for parents and police officers alike. The center is in the business of helping children. Pete Banks and his group of dedicated instructors are working around the clock to make sure everything that can be done to educate parents and law enforcement is being done. After having attended the school supervised by Pete, I had a new appreciation of just how large the problem of protecting children is. Spending a week at the center opened up my eyes to how parents and law enforcement must work together, continue with training in our communities for parents and children and police officers to help understand this new manner of victimizing our children.

On the site you can look at most of the brochures and pamphlets in an Adobe Acrobat reader. The site is there to protect children and is very gracious in allowing for the use and redistribution of their materials. When I decided to write this book they were one of the first places I called to get permission to use some of their materials. They were sensational at allowing me permission to reproduce some of their Web site and links.

However, before I give you that information, I want to include the policy for reprinting the material for the National Center for Missing and Exploited Children here so that there is no mistake about its use.

Reprint Policy for NCMEC Publications

All NCMEC publications are copyrighted materials. Any individual, organization, or entity wishing to use NCMEC's copyrighted material may do so when the:

- materials are to be used for educational, noncommercial purposes. Under no circumstances is

NCMEC's copyrighted material to be used for fund-raising purposes.

- actual use will not be presented as a sponsorship or endorsement by NCMEC of any individual, entity, product, program, or event.

- actual use will not be presented as any type of partnership or affiliated relationship between NCMEC and the reprinter.

- National Center for Missing & Exploited Children is clearly noted as the source of the information.

- intended use will not conflict with NCMEC's standards for child safety.

- reprinter will immediately discontinue use of the copyrighted material if requested to do so by NCMEC.

Questions about this policy should be forwarded to the National Center for Missing & Exploited Children's Director of Publications at the Charles B. Wang International Children's Building, 699 Prince Street, Alexandria, Virginia 22314-3175; telephone number 703-274-3900; facsimile number 703-274-2222; or e-mail reprints@ncmec.org.

As you can see, these guidelines are similar to those I asked you to keep in mind when using the Safekids PowerPoint slide presentation and workbook. As long as you are not making a profit or charging for the material, use it as much as you can to protect children.

After clicking on *Education and Resources* you will

come to this page. It lists the different areas where you can obtain additional information about each topic.

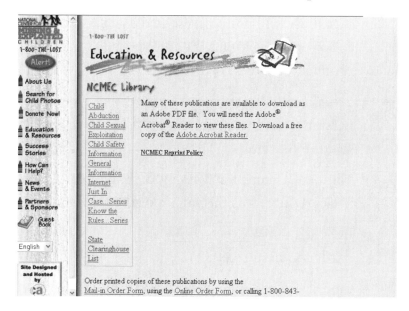

I clicked on the *Internet* tab, and the following page was displayed:

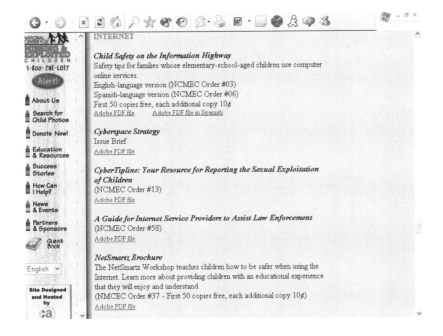

There are many more pieces of literature available to help you understand the Internet and how it affects your family. Page through the site and look at the different ones. Click on any of the PDF files, and you will open a link to the reader and be able to view the document in its entirety. You can read the document, purchase copies from the National Center, or reprint according to the policy. Take time to surf the pages. When you find something that you feel is not only good for your family, but may be helpful at your child's school, bring it to the attention of the school's administration. That is what the literature is for—getting it into the hands of the people that can do the most good with it.

One extremely important part of the National Center for Missing and Exploited Children's Web page is the ability to field complaints and make sure they are routed to the proper authorities. If you have received a graphic e-mail with content about exploiting children, click on the link to report a cyber tip.

You will be taken to this page for an assessment of the type of complaint you want to file:

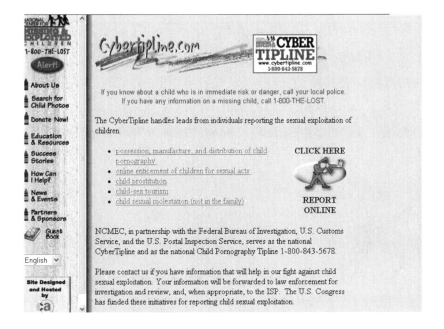

Follow the rules for reporting the crime. Remember, do not reproduce any child pornography to make the report. You can cut, copy, and paste the link from the offending e-mail or Web site and allow the staff at the National Center to do the follow-up. They will know if you are just one of many that received the e-mail or Web site, if there are others, how many, and what jurisdiction is working on solving the crime. I personally call them quite often. In fact, I hope they don't start to ignore me for calling so much. In just the last month they have helped clear up two harassment cases and two child pornography cases. Their online reporting makes a good avenue for any parent looking to make a complaint about an online crime when the local law enforcement agency just doesn't have the technology or understanding to work the case.

5 | Illinois State Attorney General's Web Site

Jim Ryan, the Attorney General of Illinois, has developed a Web site with many different ways for parents to get information about safe guarding their children. The site *www.ag.state.il.us* is full of links to very helpful material.

The page has links from assisting the public with filing a complaint to obtaining the online contract to protect your child. Right on the front page at the bottom is a link to help with home repair fraud. By clicking on the *Children's Area* you can see links to issues dealing with protecting our children. Tips on preventing and dealing with school violence or violent video or computer games.

Office of Illinois Attorney General

Children's Programs

Safe To Learn

School Violence Tipline

All Right

Violent Video Games

Illinois Youth Court Association

Sex Offender Management Board

As Attorney General, it is my belief that parents, communities, businesses, and government must all work together to protect and help the children of Illinois. In keeping with this belief, I created the Safe To Learn initiative, a long-range, statewide, coordinated approach to developing community-based programs for the promotion and preservation of children's health, safety, and education. The programs listed on this page have grown out of the Safe To Learn initiative in our efforts to continue to meet the needs of children throughout Illinois.

Clicking on the link for Programs takes us into the Family Internet Page.

FAMILY INTERNET SAFETY

Office of the Illinois Attorney General Jim Ryan

The Internet can be a fun and educational experience in many ways. New opportunities for education, entertainment and commerce are brought online every day. But while "surfing the Net" holds great promise in shaping the experiences and education of our youth, at the same time, the Internet presents many of the same dangers our children face in the real world. Just as there are people intent on harming kids at the playground, now there are people intent on harming kids at the "cyber playground." We must take reasonable precautions to make sure Illinois children have a safe, educational, and enjoyable experience on the Internet.

Online Safety Tips

Agreement to Abide by the Rules (PDF)

High Tech Crimes Bureau and Illinois Internet Child Exploitation Task Force

Illinois Computer Crime Institute

There is a link to online safety tips for parents, children, and teachers. You'll find a link to the agreement for children and parents to abide by the rules while online. You'll also be able to send in a complaint about an offensive e-mail or Web site. The complaint will be sent to the proper authority.

One other helpful Web site is the National Fraud Center page (*http://www.fraud.org/welcome.htm*). On this Web page, you can file a complaint for any type of Internet fraud—theft, scams, lotteries, stolen Beanie Babies.

Federal Law Enforcement Training Center

U.S. Department of the Treasury

www.fletc.gov

Training
Programs
Catalog
Student Bulletin

News & Events
What's New

Public Information
FOIA
Privacy Policy
Directives

About the FLETC
The Director
Our Mission
Employment
FAQs
About Us
Contents
Contact Us

6 | Other Sites of Interest to Law Enforcement

▶ 6.1 Federal Law Enforcement Training Center (FLETC)

The federal law enforcement-training center, located in Glynco, Georgia, offers training classes in computer crime investigation. The classes are available to all law enforcement agencies and space is limited. However, they try to accommodate any law enforcement officer and have on-site housing to help defray the cost of the training. Their Web site and list of classes can be found at *www.fletc.gov.*

The International Association of Computer Investigative Specialists

IACIS Home Page

Home
About Us
Contact Us
The President
Board of Directors
Membership
Sponsors
Training
Code of Ethics
Forensic Procedures
Ext Certification

About IACIS

IACIS is an international volunteer non-profit corporation composed of law enforcement professionals dedicated to education in the field of forensic computer science. IACIS members represent Federal, State, Local and International Law Enforcement professionals. Regular IACIS members have been trained in the forensic science of seizing and processing computer systems.

What's New

2002 GOLD
CORPORATE
SPONSORS

Digital Intelligence

Guidance Software

▶ 6.2 International Association of Computer Investigative Specialists

For any police officer intending to become qualified in computer forensics this school is a must. The school works in conjunction with Guidance Software, makers of the Encase software for forensic recovery of computer evidence. The software has three levels of qualification, and normally, the classes last for two weeks. In time, every police department will be working to have at least one officer certified as a computer forensic specialist and this school is a good start to getting that officer qualified. See *www.cops.org*.

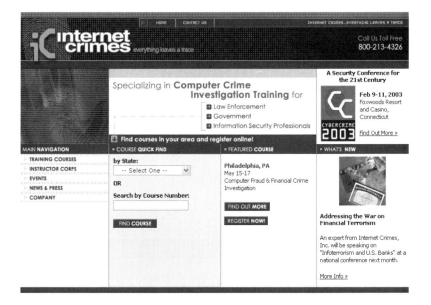

▶ 6.3 Internet Crimes, Inc.

Internet Crimes is a company based in Madison, Connecticut, that will come to your town to provide training on a wide variety of topics. The company assembles computer crimes specialists from all over the country and flies them into your location to help hold down the cost of the training by reducing the cost of travel, hotel and meals. Full time or retired law enforcement officials including local, state, and federal officers and prosecutors teach the courses.

The instruction is done in a classroom and computer lab setting to allow for hands-on demonstration of the techniques used to track, arrest and prosecute offenders using the computer and the Internet to commit computer crimes such as child exploitation, fraud, harassment, and stalking.

Home >> Training Courses

◪ TRAINING **COURSES**

Digital fraud. Electronic stalking. Online child exploitation.

These are the crimes of the 21st Century... the challenge for investigators is gathering the tools and techniques necessary to crack the cases.
Internet Crimes is the leader in computer crime investigation training. Our classes are not a lecture series. We deliver:

- Hands-on Classroom Training
- Expert Instructors
- The latest tactics for fighting High-tech criminals

Course Offerings

Computer Crime Investigator™ Certification Program

Our flagship training program, this Certification Program has been acclaimed by police investigators from across the United States. Teaches you the essential skills for computer crime investigation and online undercover operations.

◪ MORE INFO　　　　　　　◪ VIEW SCHEDULE

Computer Fraud & Financial Crime Investigation™

Learn the art of tracing electronic financial crimes—including intellectual property theft, identity swiping, and credit card fraud. Perfect for both police investigators and corporate information security professionals.

◪ MORE INFO　　　　　　　◪ VIEW SCHEDULE

Computer Child Exploitation Investigation™
Law Enforcement Only
Gain the technical skills you need to conduct undercover investigations that capture Internet pedophiles...and learn how to protect children in your community from online predators.

A complete list of the classes offered can be found at *www.internetcrimes.com.*

The **National White Collar Crime Center (NW3C)** provides support services to state and local law enforcement for the prevention, investigation, and prosecution of high-tech and economic crime. Information about NW3C may be found at:

http://www.nw3c.org

National White Collar Crime Center
Suite 300
7401 Beaufont Springs Drive
Richmond, VA 23225-5504
(804) 323-3563

The **Institute for Intergovernmental Research (IIR)** receives grant funding from the Bureau of Justice Assistance, U.S. Department of Justice, to provide management performance, policy research, technical training, and activity analysis activities for NW3C. IIR provides these research and analysis activities in the areas of:

▶ 6.4 National White Collar Crime Center

The National White Collar Crime Center provides training and support for law enforcement engaged in the investigation of high tech crimes. The training is offered to law enforcement officials to gain an understanding of the technical aspects of computer-related crimes. *www.iir.com/nwccc.htm.*

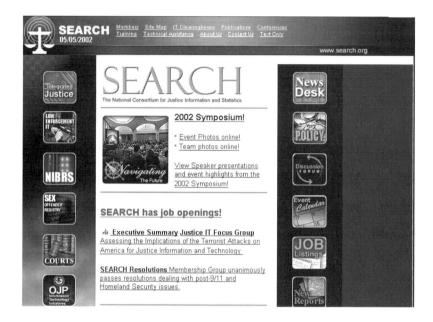

▶ 6.5 SEARCH, The National Consortium for Justice Information and Statistics

Search is a training resource for law enforcement official based in Sacramento, California. They will travel to other areas of the United States and Canada to teach classes in the investigation of high tech crimes. The courses are in-depth and very technologically involved. Visit *www.search.org*.

▶ 6.6 High Tech Crimes Investigators Association. (HTCIA)

A membership in the High Tech Crimes Investigators Association (HTCIA) is a great resource and a must for any law enforcement officer working in the area of high tech crimes. Membership in this organization allows access to some of the brightest minds in the technology field. It is not limited to just the law enforcement side of the field, as the private sector is also a member of the organization. With the crossover, any law enforcement officer would benefit greatly from being able to talk with and work with the private sector on unraveling the technology involved in committing computer crimes. Their address is *www.htcia.org*.

Index

.